BEACHCOMBING FOR BEGINNERS

NORMAN HICKIN

*With over 70 scraperboard illustrations
by the Author*

1976 EDITION

Published by
Melvin Powers
WILSHIRE BOOK COMPANY
12015 Sherman Road
No. Hollywood, California 91605
Telephone: (213) 875-1711

ISBN 0 7153 6831 1
Library of Congress Catalog Card Number 74-20446

© Norman Hickin 1975

All rights reserved. No part of this
publication may be reproduced, stored
in a retrieval system, or transmitted, in
any form or by any means, electronic,
mechanical, photocopying, recording or
otherwise, without the prior permission
of David & Charles (Holdings) Limited

Set in 12 on 13 point Bembo
and printed in Great Britain
by Redwood Burn Ltd, Trowbridge & Esher
for David & Charles (Holdings) Limited
South Devon House Newton Abbot Devon

Published in the United States of America
by David & Charles Inc
North Pomfret Vermont 05053 USA

Published in Canada
by Douglas David & Charles Limited
132 Philip Avenue North Vancouver BC

Printed by
HAL LEIGHTON PRINTING CO.
P.O. Box 1231
Beverly Hills, California 90213
Telephone: (213) 983-1105

Contents

Introduction

Many, young and old, from all walks of life take their leisure and enjoyment in walking along shores. The writer admits to being one of this number from a very early age. The freshness and the brightness of the seashore, the treading on virgin sand and often the remoteness and the freedom from man-made noise give refreshment to many, often of quite an extraordinary and exhilarating nature. No matter for what other reason the beachcomber walks the shores, he is almost certain to experience these attractions.

It is indeed a fact that many men have thrown up all their ambitions, aspirations and worldly wealth merely to roam the beaches of some sunny land. Additional to the pleasures of simple beach walking, many will enjoy the observation and the collection of the shore-dwelling and marine organisms which have been stripped from their niches by the tides and cast upon the beach.

This characteristic flora and fauna, to be picked up from the shore, have always been an essential component of a children's holiday by the sea, but they are simple pleasures that can be enjoyed by young and old alike. This constitutes the marine natural history element in beachcombing, and this book will deal exclusively with this aspect. There are so many treasures to be found in pattern, form, texture and colour amongst the animal and vegetable remains left along the tidemarks of our shores that they merit our whole attention. There are many fascinations. The beachcombing naturalist has little idea of what treasures lie in store for him when he visits a strange beach. After a wild night at sea he can make surprising discoveries even on beaches with which he is familiar. A few years ago on a South Wales beach dozens of the intricately beautiful Aristotle's Lanterns were picked up from amongst the pebbles. These are the mouthparts of sea-urchins but the globular

7

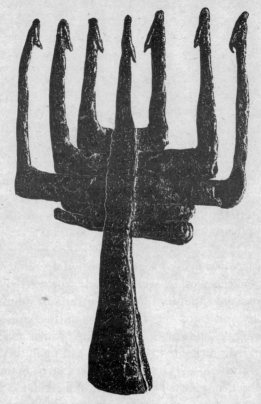

Fig 1   A fish spear from the Lipari islands
probably used for tunny fish

outer skeletal parts of the creatures were not present. It was not
until a local boatman told me that this was a popular locality for
the skin-diver that the puzzle was solved. The skin-divers merci-
lessly cut out the mouthparts from the urchin and pull out the soft
tissue as it is only the hard outer skeleton that is of value to them.
Of course, the beachcomber who collects his specimens from
antique and junk shops, and other commercial sources, cannot
know how the animals met their end.
The beachcombing novice must not think that he is the first

Fig 2 The scorpion murex, *Murex scorpio*, from the Philippines. This highly convoluted shell is 5in long

beachcomber ever. Indeed, for centuries the shores of the world have been searched in order to discover the beautiful or useful objects that have been washed ashore. A high proportion of these objects are durable. They consist of the hard parts – the bone, shell, wood, or mineralised parts of an animal or plant, the softer tissues of which have been washed away in sea water. These collectable items are now to be found in homes or used as special décor in various sorts of establishment. They have become articles of commerce and are found today in countless numbers of antique shops and stalls throughout the world. That is, those articles which have not been channelled into rather more permanent forms of exhibition such as museums, or into the décor of the more sophisticated restaurants.

A beach is not an essential environment for a beachcomber. One's beachcombing can be accomplished quite adequately along the

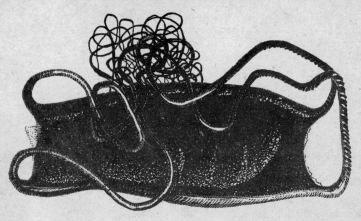

Fig 3 · Egg-case of a dogfish, *Scyliorhinus species*, from Dunmanus Bay, Ireland. Length from base of horns, 3¼in. The coiled, springy, tentacles fasten amongst the seaweeds

Portobello Road on a Saturday afternoon, or the Flea Market in Paris, or the Oriental Road in Bangkok. Shells of extraordinary variety, puffer fish, sharks' jaws, and odd pieces of coral are to be found, not amongst the quiet wind-blown sand, but scattered amongst all the other almost infinite variety of objects on the stands, stalls, and in windows of the polyglot commercial world.

One important element in beachcombing is that the beachcomber does not harm, or cause the death of, any animal or plant. The specimens he collects are dead, most having died naturally through senility, predation or accident. He collects the skeletal parts of the animals and plants when the soft tissues have been decayed and washed away. The seaweeds he collects have been torn from their anchorages by storm and therefore can take little or no further part in the living ecological pattern. The beach-comber, then, does not interfere with any living creature nor does he meddle with the balance or interplay of the animal populations of the sea and shore, and this should be his charter.

However, the beachcomber will sometimes collect the remains of creatures that have been brought to their death by human agencies. The fisherman casts away many of the unwanted sea animals

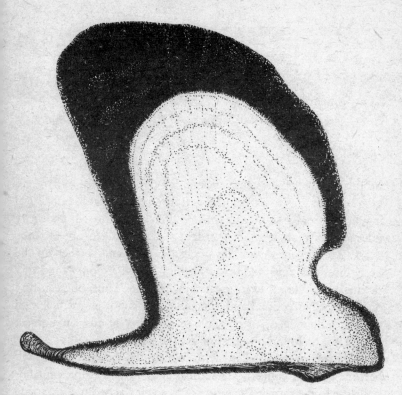

Fig 4 The unpalatable giant wing oyster is to be found in many areas of the Indo-Pacific region where it is often common. The shell is fairly fragile and the wing-like extensions often break off. The shell is up to 6in in length

which get into his nets and basket traps or become tangled in his lines. Many birds and hosts of other animals too, come to their end through contamination with oil spilled out from tankers or through the agency of other polluting factors. Many skin-divers cause wholesale destruction of a number of animal species of the shallow sea which until relatively recently lived out their lives in comparative safety from man's activity.

It is not the case, of course, that only objects of marine origin are to be found on the beaches. Indeed, most of the detritus washed

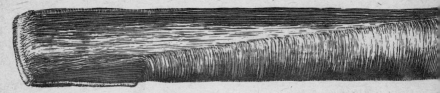

Fig 5   One valve of the shell of the razorfish, *Solen marginatus*. 4½in long;
West Wittering, Sussex

off the land by streams and rivers in flood, or dropped in by man, gets carried away towards the sea. If it remains afloat long enough it will eventually reach the sea and after being thrown about by tides and currents it is likely that it will be washed up on some shore. There, successive tides wash it further and further up the beach until a spring tide throws it high up where only the spray reaches it or tides of even greater magnitude. Thus, one can find on the beaches, animal and vegetable debris not associated with the sea and, indeed, there is no reason why almost any object should not be found on occasion on the seashore.

Another group of objects with which the beachcomber will become familiar concern the animals and plants that live on land, but close to the shore. The sand dunes particularly often support a fauna and flora which is characteristic of this type of region, but other types of shorelines are often rich in animals and plants sometimes specially adapted to live in such an ecological niche. The beachcomber will come across the remains of such animals when some mischance has overtaken them. Plant remains, after desiccation, sometimes get blown by the wind along the shores until they are far from their point of origin.

This broadens the field of knowledge to be pursued and, in fact, it can be said that the beachcomber is a naturalist of wide horizons. Some of the old books which could be of great interest and value to the beachcomber can still be found amongst the cheap book sections on second-hand bookstalls. Although the prices have risen from the sixpence and shilling range at the time I bought my copies many years ago, they are still relatively inexpensive.

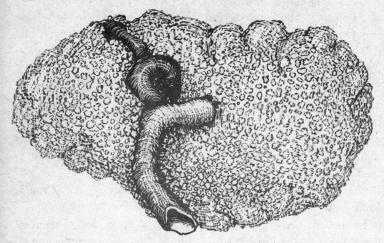

Fig 6   Tube of a serpulid worm on limestone, Rottnest island, Western Australia. Diameter of tube is over one quarter of an inch

Amongst these are Arabella Gifford's *Marine Botanist or an Introduction to the Study of the British Seaweeds*. Mine is the third edition published at Brighton by Folthorp in 1853. There are a number of line illustrations and a few very beautiful coloured plates in this little book and it has given me a great deal of pleasure. *The Seaside Book; Being an Introduction to the Natural History of the British Coasts* by W. H. Harvey has also been a great favourite of mine over many years. This contains a wealth of line drawings and was published by John Van Voorst of London. Mine is the fourth edition dated 1857.

Great fun can be obtained by beachcombing for these books about beachcombing!

There are two other old books which should be specially sought, although they are not likely to be bought cheaply. Firstly, Edward Forbes's *History of British Starfishes and Other Animals of the Class Echinodermata*. This was published by John Van Voorst of London in 1841. There are numerous woodcuts. The other is *A Manual of the Land and Fresh Water Shells of the British Islands* by William Turton. This was published by Longman, Orme, Brown, Green and Longmans in London, and my edition, revised by John Ede and Gray, is dated 1840. There are a number of beautiful hand-coloured plates, although a large number of the figures are very small.

Still to be found on second-hand bookshelves (although usually in a battered condition) are *The Ocean World* by Fiquier containing a large number of line drawings, and *A Popular History of British Zoophytes or Corallines* by D. Lansborough. This latter book was published by Reeve & Co in 1852 and contains twenty hand-coloured plates.

Rather more modern are two books of photographs by Douglas P. Wilson. They are the classic *Life of the Shore and Shallow Sea* published in 1935 by Ivor Nicholson & Watson, and *They Live in the Sea* published in 1947 by Collins.

THE BEACHCOMBER AS A CONSERVATIONIST

What a beautiful place is a beach! It is washed and scoured by the salt water dashing or flowing over it twice a day. It is therefore all the more regrettable when too great a strain is put upon the cleansing action of the sea. The beachcomber will often come across rubbish thrown overboard: half grapefruits are the most frequent objects of this nature which he encounters. The throwing of rubbish overboard at sea, even in the narrow sea-lanes such as the English Channel, is the conventional method of disposal. Hardly anyone would comment on this except the beachcomber who values the beauty of the beaches he walks along. The problem of disposal of oil at sea by the washing out of tanks and the oil leaking from ships holed or wrecked at sea is mentioned elsewhere. The landward spoliation of our beaches also can often be observed by the comber.

One method of beach destruction, often experienced, is when the beach is converted into a rubbish tip. It is appreciated that in some districts where the rock is only a few inches below the soil there are difficulties experienced in burying rubbish, but trying to put it out of sight by putting it on a beach and hoping it will be washed out to sea is a disgusting procedure. Equally disgusting and even more reprehensible on hygienic grounds, is the action by many towns and cities of dumping untreated sewage into the sea, again in the uncertain and vain hope that it will not be seen again. There is nothing more disgusting than walking along a beach onto which the contents of a town's toilets have been deposited. The other type of beach spoliation is the unofficial dumping ground. Sometimes one finds these in the most extraordinary places even along the less frequented parts of well known beaches at seaside resorts. Most usually it is garden refuse which is deposited in this way, but often refrigerators, cartons of tin cans, mattresses and even slaughter-house refuse also join the unsavoury pile.

The good beachcomber will consider himself an honorary warden of all the beaches he visits; cleaning up, burying, destroying or removing offending objects. It is rather a dismal thought that the list of the latter is a long one, but tin cans, polythene sheeting and containers, and broken glass are but a few examples. Tin cans rust and gradually disintegrate, whilst pieces of glass have the corners rubbed off and become attractive pebbles, but polythene is an abomination to those who possess any sensitivity for the beauty of the shores. It appears to be well nigh indestructible except by fire. Obviously many tasks of beach conservation would be beyond the physical powers of an individual, but not beyond those of a group of young people enthusiastically and ably led. Wholesale refuse and litter dumping should be reported to the local authority. Yes, the good beachcomber is a beach cleaner as well.

Chapter 1

The Beachcomber
and his Collection

This book is for the naturalist beachcomber seeking to identify the animal and vegetable organisms of the sea whose remains are washed up onto the shore. He will learn to associate the flora and fauna which he finds with the type of shore and with the characteristics of the nearby sea bed. He will learn something of many important groups of animals and plants which are not to be found on land. Before one can collect however, one has to learn to observe. Then, having collected, the specimens must be preserved and labelled, and then maintained. Let us commence with the ability to observe.

THE ABILITY TO OBSERVE

Perhaps one of the best exercises for training the eye to 'see' is to search a natural environment, such as a shore, for a variety of natural objects. Obviously, the eyes of every person walking along a seashore will convey a picture to the brain of all that is 'seen' but in spite of this most people would be oblivious to the natural objects that surround them on all sides. The trained observer, on the other hand, would not only be able to pick out from their background the objects for which he was searching, but he would also be aware of strange, unusual or obtruding objects. Thus, seeing is quite distinct from perceiving or observing. There is no doubt that the ability of perception or observation can be sharpened or improved by training or exercise.

I was led to ponder over these matters as long ago as 1945 when I was searching for colorado beetles in the Channel Islands. These black and yellow, gaudily striped beetles were said to be seen in

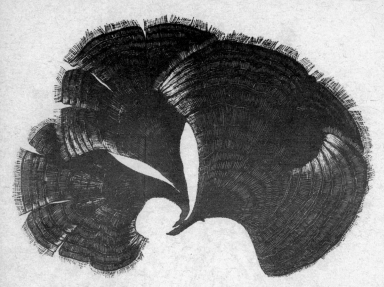

Fig 7 *Padina pavonia.* The peacock's tail seaweed is found along the south-west English coast in shallow tide-pools. It is, however, a mainly tropical species growing on coral reefs. This 'brown' seaweed is marked with concentric bands of yellowish, green and reddish-brown and white encrustations of lime. Drawn from a Victorian seaweed herbarium

thousands on one of Jersey's sandy beaches where they had been washed up by the tide. I searched and scoured the sandy tide-lines for a couple of hours in the evening before the light failed. This was completely unsuccessful. I had to leave midday the following day, but as soon as I could get out of the hotel in the morning I hurried to the same beach, checking with a map that this was, indeed, the beach which my informant had mentioned. Up and down I went for an hour or so without a glimpse of a colorado! It should be mentioned that I was familiar with the size, shape and colour of this insect, its ladybird-like shape, but half-inch size, and the longitudinal black and yellow stripes, making it unmistakable. But suddenly I saw one – its front end was buried in the sand but its striped wing cases made it easily recognisable. The strange thing was that within a minute I had

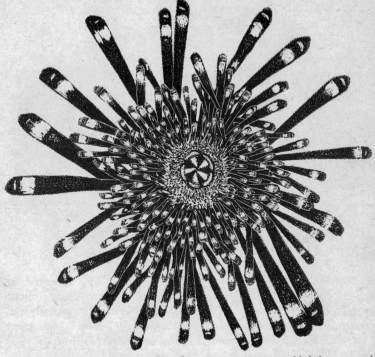

Fig 8 The club-spined sea-urchin from Mexico. It is reddish-brown and white and measures about 6in across to the tips of the spines. It must be stored carefully and *never* handled or its 'clubs' will become detached

found another, and then another, so that a few minutes after finding the first one, I had found about a hundred. Everywhere I looked on the sand I saw colorado beetles more or less covered with sand but with some part exposed. Yet previously I had searched for some hours and found none. Obviously, I had searched without bearing a picture in my mind of what I was looking for. I had looked at them many times before, but I had not 'seen' them.

This proved to me the value of observation, of seeing rather than looking, and if the beachcomber gains nothing more (and there are many other rewards) than the ability to observe what lies partly buried in the sand, then he will have gained something of value.

With observant eyes, one sometimes comes across the most extraordinary objects in one's beachcombing. Route 90 in the United States, for some miles, runs along the shores of the Mexican Gulf. Between Biloxi and Gulfport in the State of Mississippi it scarcely skirts the high-tide mark and there is an unending stream of high-powered motor cars. Although the month was October, there were a number of butterflies flying about, but as I picked my way along the sandy road's edge I noticed a dead butterfly on the ground. Close examination revealed that it was not damaged in any way, but the really remarkable thing was that in the next half a mile I found something like 100 undamaged, but dead, butterflies on the sand, not of one species but of many – the monarch, the silver-spangled gulf fritillary, and a number of others. No doubt if I had looked further I would have found many hundreds, probably thousands. There seems to be no convincing explanation to account for their death, as the delicate butterflies were totally unmarked.

A competent naturalist-observer should be able to identify every natural object that he sees. Obviously he will not be able to give every species its name nor indeed will he be able to name all the families, but in his own country or in special localities he should be able to do this in respect of groups of organisms in which he has specialised; he should be able to assign the creatures to their main groupings. It is in the field that the ability to recognise the identity of an animal or a plant becomes a rewarding asset. Many natural objects almost seem to disappear into their background more especially if the latter is rich and varied in species, although one can often be misled in this respect in such a seemingly sterile locality as a sandy shore. The number of animals of a number of different groups which can be found on and in the sand is often surprising. Of course, when the glance of a naturalist-observer rests upon any patch of the environment, the organisms present do not appear like illustrations on the page of a book. Most often only some small part of it is visible and it is this small visible part

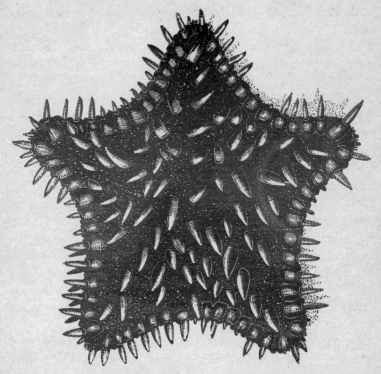

Fig 9 The horned starfish-from New Mexico. This specimen is 6in across.
It creeps slowly over rocks preying on any animal whose shells it can prise open,
and at the same time is relatively safe from predation itself

which the beachcomber must be able to recognise. If an object
puzzles him, he should seek to satisfy his curiosity.
I want to give an example of this, although it occurred in a desert
area a few hundred miles from a beach. This was the Nyenga on
the southern border of Kenya which we were traversing in order
to get to Amboseli. It was a dusty drive across the featureless
landscape and in 1958 there was no track to follow. However, at
one stopping place when I got out of the Land-Rover, my eye
alighted on a small biscuit-shaped whitish object sticking out of
the sand. It somehow seemed out of place, and even the way it

stuck out of the sand seemed rather strange. Curiosity overcame me, and I moved the sand away from it to reveal the cranium of a very old, almost fossilised, human skull. On the sandy beaches objects are often partially or wholly buried due to wave-action. The beachcomber can do little about the latter, but the former offer clues from the unburied parts that project from the sand. The shape, colour and texture of these should stimulate the beachcomber to learn what lies beneath. If he cannot identify the object from the small visible part, then he should uncover it. In this way, he will score a success over beachcombers who have walked the shore before him but whose eyes were focused only on the superficial.

COLLECTION MAINTENANCE

The first essential for the preservation of one's collection of beachcombing material is to maintain it in a thoroughly dry condition. Many organic materials such as seaweeds will quickly deteriorate if allowed to get damp. Even seemingly permanent specimens such as bivalve molluscs can suffer damage in this through the ligament being caused to rot. Preferably the material should be stored in a centrally heated room. If this is not possible, then the specimens should be exposed to good ventilation on open shelves. In this way the specimens are able to tolerate a greater degree of humidity without deterioration than if they were enclosed in tin boxes in conditions of high humidity.

THE STORAGE OF THE COLLECTION

Subject to what has been stated above, it is obviously a good principle to store the collection in such a way that the specimens can be seen. A glass-fronted cabinet or bookcase is excellent. The writer's own collection is mainly stored in perspex boxes. This has been especially advantageous in that fragile specimens can be drawn without their being handled.

It is extremely important to clean all shells, bones, and other

21

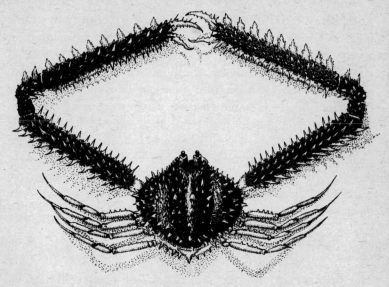

Fig 10 The claw-legs of this crab from Bangkok have developed to an extraordinary extent. They are heavily armoured with spinous projections as is the top of the carapace but the walking legs and underside of abdomen are white and soft

skeletal specimens thoroughly. All vestiges of soft visceral or muscular tissue must be removed. The cleaner such specimens are, the longer will they remain without damage in a humid atmosphere. So long as the specimens are maintained in a bone-dry condition they will come to little harm. On the other hand, if they become damp they will almost certainly become infested by mites, psocids, or house-moth larvae. Although none of these creatures will actually damage the shell or bone, they cause a lot of mess making the specimens dusty and unattractive. House-moth and clothes-moth larvae will attack feathers and damage them severely, although they tend to be attracted mostly to soiled feathers. It is desirable to give all feathers a light spray with an insecticide of the long lasting kind. Allow this to dry thoroughly before mounting feathers on card, otherwise oily patches may result.

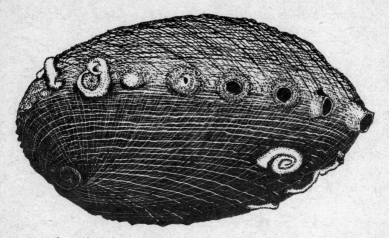

Fig 11 The red abalone, *Haliotis rufescens*, is found along much of the Californian coast. It is a large species growing up to 12in in length. The specimen illustrated is from Monterey

If it is essential to pack the specimens in boxes, then special precautions must be taken to prevent damage. Bivalve mollusc shells should be tied together with cotton so that even if they become separated they are associated. Newspaper is quite good for wrapping, but two layers should be used. The first should be tightly wrapped around the specimen and the second should be only loosely wrapped and folded and crimped also, so that it is quite springy. Specimens with projections should have the projections wrapped separately. Polythene bags are also very useful for general handling or storage of the specimens, but reliance should not be placed on this method for transporting through the post. However, the polythene bag is useful for associating notes and information with the specimen if the bag is afterwards fastened up with a wire-papered strip sold for the purpose. Incidentally, if an object such as a starfish has dried in a contorted manner, it is often possible to soften it by soaking in water for about 24 hours, then drying it again after pulling it into the desired position. The drying operation can be carried out between sheets of dry blotting paper or newspaper – changing it from time to time.

LABELLING

Whatever the reason for making the collection, if it is properly labelled it gains immeasurably in value from the scientific point of view. It may be that you might think the objects you have collected from the shore are of little value, but the moment you have labelled them they become scientific facts. There are three essential features of a label which satisfy technical considerations. In the first place, the date on which the specimen was collected must be stated. Secondly, the place of collection is important and this must be given with enough detail to enable another collector to seek out the exact spot. Secrecy must not be in your mind. Your specimen may possibly give rise to scientific interest to someone who may want to record it and no one would do this if there was no indication where the specimen came from. If your beachcombing ranges over the world then obviously the country in which you collected it should be stated. If you do not know the name of your beach then identify it by the distance from a well known place. If all else fails a map reference or its latitude and longitude should be given. Lastly, the name of the collector should be stated. Again, this is most important information if any investigator wished to follow up the circumstances of the specimen's collection.

Now, the beachcombing beginner, at this point, is likely to ask where and how all this information is to be given. With an insect on a pin there is no difficulty, the essential information, the data, is impaled on the same pin as the insect, so there is no problem of dissociation. With specimens preserved in alcohol, the data is written on a slip of paper in indian ink and placed *inside* the bottle or jar with the specimens. Such a label would never be stuck on the outside of the jar as it would certainly become unstuck with the passage of years. The nature of a large pro-portion of beachcombed specimens makes possible the direct application of the data. Select a smooth, clear patch on the specimen and, of course, write the data legibly – preferably in block capitals – directly onto the specimen. Indian ink applied with a mapping pen is one of the best methods but a black ball-point pen can be used if the former is not available. You might have to smooth a small area if the specimen is rough, using sandpaper or a chisel, and if it is dark in colour then whiten the patch with a little paint. This data patch should be in an unobtrusive part of the specimen, where it will not be seen unless specially searched for. This method is usually applicable to shells, bones, large crustaceans, and wood, but may not be appropriate for other specimens such as seaweeds or feathers. In these cases the data label should be made of a small piece of stiff, strong card, and should be fastened to the specimen with wire or strong twine. If the specimen is fragile and kept in a box then the label should be kept inside. You may want to write another label for the box but this should be additional to, and not in place of, the label *inside* the box.

Another method of labelling specimens is to write a number on the specimen and to keep a notebook with the data of collection written against the number in the book.

This method is not to be recommended. There are many collections of neatly numbered specimens of various sorts where the notebook has been lost or destroyed. Similarly, there are notebooks known where there is no knowledge of the location of the collection. The direct association of the specimen with the data is not only desirable, it is essential. The little bit of extra trouble is well worth while.

Chapter 2

The Weeds of the Sea

A very large number of the organisms living in the sea belong to the vegetable kingdom and are generally known as seaweeds. From the evolutionary point of view they are amongst the most primitive of plants, and belong to the group known as the *Algae*, in which the organs and the tissues show only a very simple differentiation. The broad ideas concerning classification of plants and animals in which progression is made from the relatively simple organisms to those relatively more complex, will be familiar (to a greater or lesser degree) to the reader, and this is the arrangement followed in this account. However, in any account of plants and animals the use of scientific names is often off-putting, and yet the author is almost always obliged to use them. The reason for the reader's dislike of these latinised names is largely due to his belief that they are to be pronounced! This is far from the case. In the vast majority of cases they are read only, almost as registration or index numbers. Many of the groups of organisms, and even more of species, possess no common names in English, or they may be called a variety of names according to the different regions of the country. It is hoped, therefore, that the reader will excuse the use of scientific names here and there, so that the reader who desires to further his study of any group will know precisely what it is called.

THE ALGAE CLASSIFICATION

The seaweeds or algae, are grouped in a number of classes within the main division *Thallophyta*. A small number of species, but including a few well known ones, are classified within the green algae or *Chlorophyceae*. The sea lettuce, *Ulva lactuca*, belongs here. The strands, which are flat and leaf-like, and are only two cells in

Fig 12   *Ulva linga*, the sea lettuce is bright green and is an early coloniser of rock
pools exposed to bright sunlight

thickness, are joined at the base. *Enteromorpha* is another genus of
pure green seaweed but, in general, there are few marine species in
this group. A number of species of seaweeds are to be found in the
order *Siphonales* and include the feathery *Cladophera*, and the
Mediterranean *Caulerpa prolifera* which has all the appearance of
possessing leaves and roots, although these highly specialised
organs are not developed in the algae. It is, however, in the
brown algae or *Phaeophyceae* that we find the majority of the
well known seaweed species around European shores.

Fig 13 The brown seaweed *Taonia atomaria* has fan-shaped fronds with irregular clefts and is marked with delicate concentric lines. Southern and eastern coasts of England

It is in the *Fucales* that we see dominant species along the rocky coast-line of northern Europe. A number of species of *Fucus* are amongst the best known of all seaweeds. These are often called 'wracks'. The thallus is dichotomously branched and ribbon-shaped. Bladderwrack, *Fucus vesiculosus*, bears air bladders near the tips of the thallus branches and this, as well as other species of the genus, attach themselves very firmly to rocks by a disc-shaped holdfast. The weed of the Sargasso Sea belongs to this group but shows an advanced differentiation as the branchlets exhibit various functions, including that of floating organs similar to bladder-wrack. It is due to the possession of these that the weed is carried by ocean currents to the area. There it is to be found floating in great rafts.

The brown algae are characterised by their brown colouration. Green chlorophyll is present but is masked by a number of other dark-coloured pigments, especially by Fucoxanthin. These brown pigments are soluble in alcohol so that this can be demonstrated by washing the brown seaweed in some alcohol, when it turns to a bright green colour. One of the most widely distributed species is *Ectocarpus siliculosus*. *Dictyota dichotoma* is found throughout the European coastline. The ribbon-shaped thallus branches dichot-omously as its name implies. The group known as the *Laminariales* is remarkable for containing the largest of the algae. *Macrocystis pyrifera* which is found in antarctic waters grows up to a length of 70 metres. *Lessonia*, is another antarctic genus, the main axis of which is said to grow to a thickness equal to that of a man's thigh! Most beachcombers along the Atlantic and North Sea coasts would have noticed the oar-weed at low tide. These are species of *Laminaria*. There is a root-like holdfast, a stalk-like axis, and a broad, expanded, ribbon-like thallus which may be several metres in length. When this part of the weed has rotted, the holdfasts (often attached to the axis) sometimes accumulate in large drifts along the high-tide mark, and they dry to a tough leathery con-sistency. They often assume beautiful shapes and can be collected by the beachcomber for inclusion in décor. Sometimes the hold-fasts cling tightly to a stone or a number of pebbles or shells and are curious and attractive items.

We now come to the red algae or *Rhodophyceae*. These, also, are often a familiar sight on British beaches, especially after rough weather when they have been torn from their anchorage. Even at Wittering in Sussex, not a long drive from London, the shore is

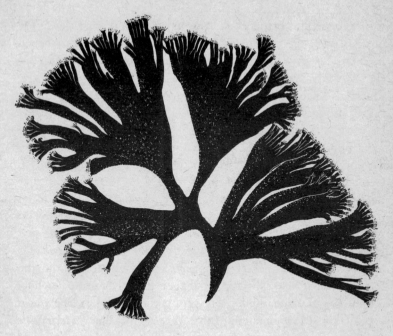

Fig 14 *Cutleria multifida.* This olive or rusty coloured 'brown' seaweed has the fronds irregularly divided but in a characteristic manner. Mainly found around British southern coasts in from 4 to 15 fathoms. Named after Miss Cutler, an early British algologist. Drawn from a Victorian seaweed herbarium

often strewn with several species. The red algae, as one might expect, are characterised by their distinctive colour. Mostly, they are red or violet but some species have a dark purplish or reddish-brown tinge. The special colouration of this group of algae is due to the presence of either the red pigment phycoerythrin, or in addition a blue pigment called phycocyanin. A few species, however, do not produce their own carbohydrate nutrients, but are parasitic on other algae. Although a few species are found in freshwater, the great majority are marine.

Chondrus crispus, found round the British coasts, has a branched ribbon-like thallus as has *Gigantina mamillora* with its warty cystoccarps. *Delesseria sanguinea* has a more complicated structure

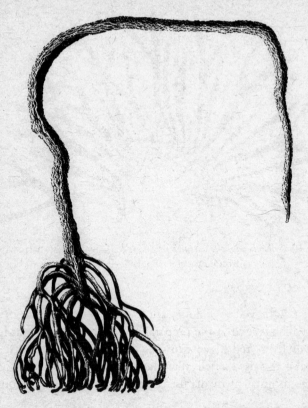

Fig 15 Extensive beds of oar-weeds (*Laminaria*) are to be found around almost the whole of the British coast just below low-tide mark except in mud and sand. After severe storms in late autumn and winter, they are often cast up onto the shore, where the blade disintegrates but the holdfast remains, drying into extraordinary contorted shapes

with the thallus modified into leaf-like organs. This species, found around many of the coasts bordering on the Atlantic, was very popular with the Victorian seaweed pressers, as was *Dudresnaya coccinea*, whose inclusion in the seaweed book had something of a status symbol about it as it was to be found mainly around the Mediterranean coastline.

The first two species mentioned above, when dried (when they

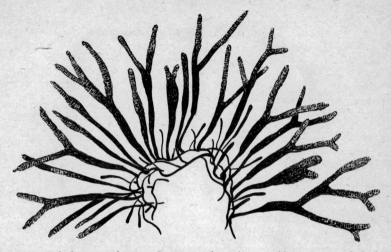

Fig 16   *Rhodymenia palmetta var. nicaensis.* This red seaweed bears narrow, forked
fronds on a creeping, root-like base

assume a light yellow colour) are known as carragheen, or Irish
moss, which is used in the preparation of jellies. Agar-agar is also
prepared from red algae growing in Far Eastern waters. This
material is also used in jelly manufacture and, in addition, has given
its name to nutrient media used in microbiological techniques.

SEARCHING AMONGST THE SEAWEED

Often after severe storms great masses of seaweeds are torn from
the seabed and thrust high upon the shore. Sometimes one might
forget the existence of extensive beds of oar-weeds just below the
low-tide mark, but at some seaside towns the fact is brought home
only too obviously when the extraordinary heaps begin to decay.
In some areas around the British coasts such accretions of decaying
seaweed perform the very important function of coast stabilisation
(that is, of course, looking at it from a purely anthropomorphic
point of view). As an example, at Worthing on the Sussex coast,
the high-water mark consists of a steep bank of shingle; when the
oar-weed is lashed onto it by the ton it sticks, so that when the

Fig 17 *Kalymenia reniformis*. This blood-red seaweed bears kidney-shaped lobes on its leaflike frond. It is thick and fleshy and grows just below low-water mark or in deep pools

shingle rolls onto it at the next high tide or during an even moderate storm, it is roughly held in position. Then as the weed decays and the sticky alginates cause the weed to hold together, so the shingle is held in place. The end result is that a *larger* shingle bed exists than was present before, and (this is the important thing from the beachcomber's point of view) a host of smaller organisms which have relied upon the forest of oar-weed for shelter and food are also present.

In spite of the great bulk of seaweed that flourishes around the shores of many countries of the world, it has little direct economic value. In the past, certain species have been used as a source of the element iodine which was made from the ashes. Some species are eaten, such as the laver or laver-bread of South Wales, and in recent years some commercial exploitation has taken place of the abundant seaweeds of the Scottish coasts. These are processed and one product is alginic acid and its salt, sodium alginate, which is used as a thickening material in liquids.

COLLECTING AND PRESERVING SEAWEEDS

During Victorian times collecting and preserving seaweeds was a popular pastime. Like many of the hobbies of that period preserving seaweeds is actually quite a simple operation requiring only very little care. However, one or two simple rules must be observed. The first is that it is impossible to make a satisfactory job of preserving a seaweed that has already been dried on the beach. It really is essential to start with fresh seaweed that has never been out of the sea. The best time to make the collection is in October when the first autumn gales have wrenched numbers of varieties from their growing positions in deeper water. Keep the seaweeds in sea water until it is convenient to work upon them. What is needed next is a flat tray in which the specimen is placed in sea water and washed. A sheet of stout paper or card is then placed in the tray and the seaweed floated onto it in the position it is desired to mount the specimen. The card is slowly removed from the tray, and tilted sideways to allow the excess water to drain away.

If the cards of mounted seaweeds are then dried between botanical drying paper (white blotting paper or even newspaper will suffice at a pinch), the specimens will adhere to the cards. When the card is perfectly dry, do not forget to write the full data, locality, date, collector etc on it. If you can get an expert to name your seaweed, add that too.

Chapter 3

The Woody Tissues of Plants

It is characteristic of many of the higher plants that some part of their tissues become woody. The cell walls become thickened and lignified, so that the tissues are dense and hard. Compared with an alga or herbaceous plant the woody parts of such plants are durable, remaining as a sort of skeletal tissue long after the fleshy parts have disintegrated. Indeed, the inner heartwood of trees is dead tissue even when the tree is living. The living part of the wood is the outer sapwood and as this contains the living cell contents with accumulated nutrients, and the nutrient sap, it will be readily appreciated that this is the part of the wood most subject to decay by fungi and the borings of wood-destroying insects and other creatures. Almost all of the woody tissues of the 18,000 or so trees and shrubs float on the sea, a fact of the greatest significance when the populating of the ocean islands of the world is contemplated. Wood as a raw material has played an enormous part in the development of man's civilisation. The dugout canoe, the wheel and almost every sort of tool had some wooden component. The controlled use of fire has been said to have been of the greatest significance, and this must have been through the use of wood as a fuel. Again the natural material which has, perhaps, appealed most to man's aesthetic senses, is wood.

Branches that have been torn asunder from the parent trunk, or roots that have been wrenched from the ground during storm or flood, are sent on their journey to the sea. Here, the bark and the non-durable sapwood is decayed by many organisms that have been mentioned, and are washed away by the action of the waves. The result is an extraordinary array of pieces of wood scattered around the coasts of the world. No two are alike, but many of them are valued for their great artistic appeal. The Japanese showed the way in which such fragments of water-worn wood

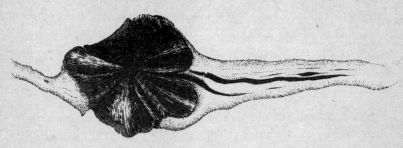

Fig 18   A rose-like gall formation of a tree root caused by a fungus in New
Zealand. These can sometimes be found as souvenir items in tourist shops

could be utilised in floral decoration. Today, however, wood is
used on a very large scale for many decorative purposes. One of
the most important of these is for window dressing, and many
architects of modern homes have used large branches or tree
trunks which have been cast upon the beach, as a central natural
aesthetic theme in order to soften the stark hard square line of
their architecture. On some shores such wooden branches are to be
found in great abundance. The beachcomber, having found a
branch which he considers most beautiful, finds another even more
delectable one, a few yards further on. An island beach near
Nelson in New Zealand proved such an *embarras de richesse*.
Here the giant tangled mass of silver-grey branches and trunks lay
in places 10ft high, and lined the shore for several miles. I tried to
tug a piece here and there but it was completely intertwined. I
gave up trying and walked along it until I was out of sight of my
companions. I just contemplated it and enjoyed the gigantic beauty
of colour and form; perhaps one of the greatest natural displays
of water-worn wood in the world.

THE WOODY PEAR

To me, probably the most beautiful and the most intriguing of all
the botanical specimens of the woody type that I have ever
collected, were the Woody Pears at the little seaside place of

36

Fig 19   Eight fruits of the woody pear, *Xylomelum angustifolium*, from Busselton, Western Australia. Each fruit is over 2in long

Busselton in Western Australia. These are the fruits of the five species of the genus *Xylomelum* in the *Proteacae* family. I am not a botanist and I must say that I thought that this family of flowering plants was restricted to South Africa. When I first journeyed to Australia, I found I was mistaken. One was first shown to me by the botanist wife of an entomologist in Canberra. This woody fruit is of shape and size of a smallish pear but stalked at the larger end. It is dehiscent, splitting longitudinally and vertically to release the two winged seeds. Dehiscence occurs only after a forest-fire. The surface of the woody pear is like velvet.

I left Canberra determined to find specimens so that I could draw them. I was so intrigued with their shape and texture that I wanted to try and capture it on scraperboard. Arming myself with the botanical details of the shrubs and trees as we journeyed around Australia, I looked and looked. As we drove through the forests I stopped and searched everywhere, but they escaped me.

After travelling through the wonderful Jarrah and Karri forests of Western Australia, I gave up hope of ever finding the **pears**. Our road back to Perth took us through the little seaside town of Busselton, and here we decided to have a cup of tea. At the edge of the beach was a little café and in we went for refreshment. It was not a very imposing place, mainly of formica and chromium plate, but when we filed out afterwards I became rooted to the ground. There in a large vase of plastic flowers and ferns was a branch covered with woody pears. I examined them closely as I thought at first they also might be made of plastic but, no, they were the real thing. I asked to see the boss and I explained my interest in his specimens. To my great surprise he not only knew what they were, but he even knew the species, *Xylomelum angustifolium*. In addition he sensed my covetous thoughts, and he reacted most generously by giving the whole branch to me. I happily bore it off, although I had to break it up into a number of clusters to get them back to England. But it was strange that I should search fruitlessly for a forest specimen in the forest, and then have my efforts crowned with success on the beach.

THE SEA BEAN

For many centuries large kidney-shaped seeds of a leguminous West Indian tree, *Entada gigas*, have been found on the western coasts of Europe, from northern France to northern Norway. In Peter Claussen's book, *Description of Norway*, published in 1632, he refers to them as 'stones floated on the sea' and they were also known as 'adder-stones' and 'eagle-stones'. In 1673, however, a book written by Provost Lucas Jacobsen Debes and published at Copenhagen called *Faeroe Revealed*, gave the opinion that they were seeds from the West Indies that were 'brought hither by the stream'. Although their true nature had been revealed so long ago, they were thought, during the eighteenth century, to be the fruits

Fig 20   The seed of the leguminous tree *Entada gigas*. On left, from the side, on right, from below, to show the point of attachment to the pod or hilum. This seed measures about 2in in length

of marine plant-like organisms such as the 'sea-fans'. A point of great interest concerning these seeds is the superstitions that grew up around them. They were used as amulets or charms by the peoples of the Hebrides, the Orkneys and the Shetlands, to ward off the evil eye and, in addition, had a number of medicinal properties ascribed to them. To some extent it is said that these beliefs still linger amongst northern villagers, but everywhere they have been washed up they have been used as snuff boxes, tinder-boxes and matchboxes.

The seeds are large, my own specimen picked up at Reenmore, Dunmanus Bay in south-west Ireland, measures 5cm by 4.5cm. It is kidney-shaped with an attachment scar or 'hilum' situated in a small concavity. In colour it is a dark purplish-brown, in fact, kidney-coloured, and is exceptionally hard.

Apparently the seed, when fresh, is heavier than sea water, but when it dries it becomes much lighter and able to float upon the sea. It is carried by the Gulf Stream to Europe in company with a number of other seeds, and it takes about a year to do this, on the current known as the West Indian Drift. Indeed it was the casting of these woody reeds upon the coasts of northern Europe that gave our early navigators the idea that there were 'streams' in the sea.

All who desire to read further upon this fascinating subject should read H. B. Guppy's works.

Chapter 4

Sponges, Corals and Jellyfish

Sponges and corals are of special interest to the beachcomber in that practically all the members of these two important groups of animals are marine, living only in sea water.

For many years the sponges were an enigma to zoologists. It was originally thought that a sponge was a colonial form of a unicellular or protozoan animal. Today, although placed next to the *Protozoa*, the sponges (or *Porifera*, as they are scientifically termed) are classified in the *Metazoa*, or many-celled animals.

In the animal kingdom then the sponges are the most primitive creatures, that is, the least differentiated, which the beachcomber is likely to meet along the shore.

It is, of course, the familiar bath sponge which most would have in mind when seeking to describe the creature. But this does give a general picture of the appearance of a sponge, and also its important property of being able to absorb a large quantity of liquid and then to expel it again on being compressed. The many descriptions of the sponge, what they were and how they lived, from the time of Aristotle, makes fascinating reading, but we can here only mention Robert Grant who in 1825 described how the sea water entered the sponge by a large number of small holes and left through a smaller number of large holes. The former are known as 'ostia' and the latter 'oscula'.

The skeletal part of the sponge, that which the beachcomber will usually find, is of great complexity and shows enormous variation amongst the various kinds of sponge. In all cases the skeletal tissue consists of interwoven fibres or spicules of various patterns. These may be of a material known as spongin or there may also be present spicules of a siliceous material. Sometimes the spongin fibres may be absent or the spicules may consist of calcium carbonate.

The beachcomber should bear in mind that the 'loofah' sponge is indeed *not* a sponge but the fibrous tissue of the fruit of a plant in the *Cucubitacae* family, which includes vegetable marrow and cucumber. All sponges are aquatic, the vast majority being marine, a very few species of a small number of genera only being found in freshwater. The sponges offer much difficulty to the beach-comber for their ready recognition on account of their great variation in shape and the apparent absence of organs by means of which they can be identified. Indeed, there are no organs of locomotion, no organs of sense or recognisable organs of sex and almost always no definite symmetry. It has been said that a sponge can be identified by these negative characters. They may be fixed or be quite free on the sea bed, but all require a current of water to flow through the various cavities and instertices of the sponge body in order to bring in oxygen for respiration and food, and in order to remove carbon dioxide and faecal material. This is accomplished by large numbers of whip-like cells which by their movement cause the water currents.

Whereas most sponges are of medium size, some attain gigantic proportions. The Neptune's cup sponge, *Raphiophora patera*, found in the vicinity of Singapore may be 3 or 4ft in height. Obviously in some parts of the world some selection will have to be made in respect of transport home. But mostly the species that one finds are easy enough to handle and their general elastic nature means that they will come through a certain amount of rough handling.

Several hundred species of sponge are known from around the British coasts and it should be easy for the beachcomber to make a small collection from those found washed up onto the shores. On the whole these are not strikingly beautiful, which contrasts strongly with the extraordinary deep sea species of the group *Hexactinellida*. The skeleton of these is made up of long glassy spicules often seeming to be delicately woven in beautiful patterns. A number possess a tuft of long spicules at the base which serve to anchor the sponge onto the sea floor. One such is *Euplectella aspergillam*, Venus's flower-basket, which is illustrated. Another

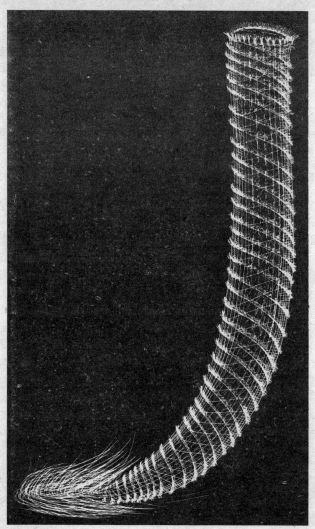

Fig 21 The Venus's flower basket, *Euplectella aspergillum*, is the name given to the Siliceous skeleton of a sponge found in deep water near the Philippines. The long glass-like spicules at the base serve to anchor it to the muddy sea-floor

species in the genus, *monoraphis*, is said to possess a single giant spicule, 9ft in length and 'of the thickness of the little finger'.

CORALS

Coral is the name given to the externally secreted limestone in its many specific forms produced by the coral polyps. In form and structure these are very like sea anemones, indeed they are grouped together and called *Zoantharia*. In these animals the tentacles and the internal cavity divisions are in groupings of six and may be numerous, although in a related group of coral polyps known as the *Alcyonaria* there are eight tentacles which are branched and there are eight internal partitions in the cavity of the polyp. Although there are a number of solitary corals (one is found on the Devon coast) most show some form of colonial organisation. This takes the form of communicating canals between the internal cavities of the polyps. However, the beachcomber will come across little, if any, remnants of the living animals but the limestone and, in some species, a horn-like material will often make up a most beautiful collection of specimens if not in the temperate climes, then on those shores where the temperature of the water seldom falls below 70°F.

Although the many species of coral polyps are so similar to each other, the corals they form are so entrancingly different. More than that, the minute granules of horn and chalk secreted and passed to the outside of the myriads of delicate polyps have made an outstanding contribution to the formation of land. The coral reefs of tropical areas are well known to almost everyone. The fringing reefs are corals which grow only at a short distance from the shore, and these can be seen from or within wading distance of the shore at low tide. Barrier reefs on the other hand, lie parallel to the coast but separated by a deep channel and, indeed, the distance of reef from shore may be several miles. Captain Cook's voyage between the Great Barrier Reef and the Queensland coast of Australia in 1770 was a fascinating exploit. He sailed about 600 miles and didn't learn of its existence until he hit it!

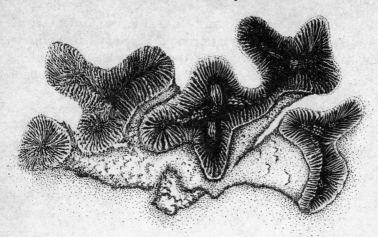

Fig 22   The reef-building corals of the warm seas have played a part of extraordinary importance in converting calcium salts in solution in the sea to dry land. This process can be seen in operation today in many tropical seas wherever reefs are in actual growth. The specimen illustrated is a 'stony' coral measuring 8in across

The third type of major coral formation is the atoll. This is a ring-shaped island formed of dead coral and usually with living coral on its outer steep slopes into the sea. The coral atoll is a characteristic feature of the South Pacific. The commonly accepted theory accounting for their presence is that of Charles Darwin who realised that in the Pacific atoll area, the land was gradually sinking. If islands which possessed fringing reefs were sinking at a rate no faster than the coral could grow, then when the island finally disappeared, its position would be marked by the circular reef – the atoll. As mentioned above, the coral is formed in an extraordinary number of differing structures according to species although the polyps themselves are of remarkable similarity.

One of the most colourful and strangely shaped corals is the organ-pipe coral. At the same time, it is one of the most important of the reef building corals of the Pacific. It is of a deep blood-red colour and takes the form of a number of distinct tubes or pipes of limestone all running in a vertical direction, joined at intervals by horizontal platform-like structures. It is in these latter that the canals joining the various members of the colony run. Normally, of course, we only see the dead coral, but in life the organ-pipe coral polyps each occupy a vertical pipe and are bright green in colour.

However, all the ramifications of corals and coral species are too many to be dealt with adequately here and what follows are a few brief notes about some of the more well known forms or those of outstanding interest.

PRECIOUS CORAL

The *Alcyonaria* with their eight tentacled polyps contains perhaps the most well known of all corals, at least in Europe, precious coral. The hard, red, calcareous core of this animal colony has been known and sought for as an adornment for women since the earliest times. Yet its true nature was not known until Jean Andre de Peyssonnel demonstrated its animal origin in the first half of the eighteenth century. Dioscorides and Pliny and hosts of later authors had previously believed it to be of plant origin, and actually de Peyssonnel, who was born at Marseilles in 1694, gave up his study of natural history to become a naval surgeon in the West Indies because of the bitterness engendered by his scientific discovery. The coral is composed of two distinct parts, the axial part of all the branches which is brittle and stony (the precious coral of commerce) and the outer covering which is soft and fleshy. This is the part which is living and the polyps are contained within protuberances in the eight clefts on the summit of each branch. When the polyp expands, the clefts open to release it. Before leaving the subject it is interesting to note what Ralph Buchsbaum wrote in connection with corals from the Great Barrier Reef: 'These dried and bleached skeletons are beautiful and are used as ornaments. But they give about as good an impression of the exquisite beauty of living expanded corals as one would get of the beauty of a woman from her whitened bones.'

FUNGIA

One is more likely to find specimens of this coral of the madrepore group whilst beachcombing in antique shops than on the shoreline. It is so named because of its resemblance to an upturned mushroom in that slender vertical lamellae radiate from the centre. When living, the polyps emerge from amongst the lamellae. *Fungia* coral has always been a curiosity and used as a house ornament, and in ancient times was thought to come from the Nile. There are a number of species however, found in various localities in the Pacific and Indian oceans, and *Fungia patella* inhabits the Red Sea. This species possesses curious worm-like polyps the apices of which have a sucker-like appearance. A number of similar fossil forms are known of Paleozoic age.

JELLYFISH

Fifteen feet below the surface of the water at Bermuda has been likened to a coelenterate jungle. This is because the gorgonians, the masses of colourful coral, and the kaleidoscopic extended discs of the sea anemones all belong to the phylum of animals known as the *Coelenterata*. This name literally means 'hollow stomach' and refers to the typical feature of this group in that the main body of the animal forms a large bag into which the captured food is stuffed, digested and also passed out afterwards through the same orifice as that through which it entered. Although there are a few coelenterates to be found in freshwater, the vast majority are marine. As previously mentioned, they are often dominant organisms. Most are rather small, although some are medium size such as jellyfish, and a few species are gigantic.

Coelenterates display two main structural forms – firstly, the medusa, which is disc-shaped with downwards trailing tentacles and is what we usually term a 'jellyfish' (this form is free floating, or can swim by taking in water then expelling it rather more forcibly), and secondly, the polyp. In this form, the mouth-fringed tentacles are uppermost and it is usually fixed or can only move very slowly by cartwheeling or edging its foot along the rock or stone which it is grasping. Many coelenterates show an alternation of these forms, one or the other predominating. Although the jellyfish are often stranded on the shore in considerable numbers, there is seldom anything for the beachcomber to collect. But on one occasion a jellyfish held special interest. We were sitting on the sands on the Norfolk coast when the children were young. As lunch was being prepared they ran off across the extensive sands as the tide was out. I could see that something held Verney's interest and she then returned to say that a jellyfish had little creatures jumping on it. On investigation, it was found that there were a large number of small crustacean species of unknown identity. Some were collected and sent to Douglas Wilson at the Plymouth Marine Biological Station. They were subsequently found to be of a species new to British waters, but known as a parasite of jellyfish in arctic regions.

Chapter 5

Starfish, Sea-urchins and their Relations

The finding of his first starfish and sea-urchins must be one of the earliest recollections of every beachcomber, but the thrill of discovering animals so totally different to those found on land is one which never really leaves him.

The starfish (*Asteroidea*), sea-urchins (*Echinoidea*), brittle-stars (*Ophiuroidea*), feather-stars (*Crinoidea*), and the sea-cucumbers (*Holothuroidea*), although differing from each other superficially to an amazing degree are, nevertheless, classified together as the phylum *Echinodermata* principally because of their radial symmetry. Most animals exhibit, to a greater or lesser extent, what is called bilateral symmetry. By that is meant, quite simply, that there is a head end and a tail end, and if a line is drawn between them the two halves which the line bisects will be similar although of 'opposite hands'. In the starfish, sea-urchins and their allies, on the other hand, the body is organised in such a way that it is accommodated into five radially arranged arms. In the starfish and brittle-stars this is very evident even to the casual observer, but in the sea- and heart-urchins a rather closer examination would have to be made. In addition to the radial arrangement of the body another common feature shared by the members of this group is the presence of a hard external skeleton. This consists of a number of calcareous plates which in the sea- and heart-urchins fit closely together to form a hard continuous shell-like structure. Spines are often present also in these latter groups conveying a high degree of protection to the animal against predation. All species in the *Echinodermata* are marine, and on account of the peculiar complexity of a number of their organs, and their adaptation to life in a number of different marine environments, they never fail to

Fig 23   The knobbed starfish from the warm coastal water of Kenya

hold the interest of the true beachcomber.

The sun-stars are rather flattened starfish with the central circular disc comparatively large. In addition the number of arms is usually greater than found in the starfish. The common British sun-star *Solaster papposus* has up to thirteen arms and is rose and purple or red and white in colour. Sun-stars of various species are quite common in many parts of the world and dried specimens are often seen in the tourist shops. Like the starfish, the cushion-stars are five-rayed but the arms are short and the central body part correspondingly large. A British species is *Porania pulvillus* which is red and orange-yellow.

Starfish and brittle-stars often lose an arm when a bivalve mollusc

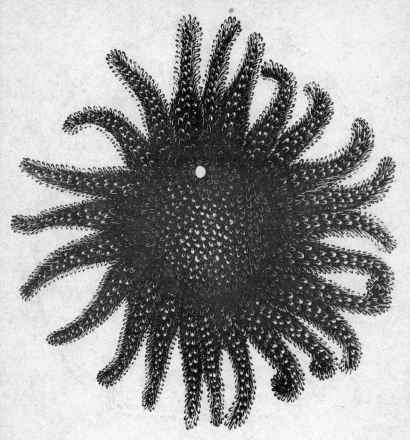

Fig 24 A sun-star from the Pacific coast of Mexico. This bluish-green species is
from 4 to 5in in length

is able to shut its valve tight on it. But these animals are able to
regenerate limbs in a quite remarkable way. Sometimes a starfish
is found with only one original arm, the other four being
regenerating ones.

The heart-urchins are similar to the sea-urchins in general shape
being somewhat globular, but as their popular name implies, they
are heart-shaped. In addition, the mouth is on the underside of the
animal whilst the anus is situated at the end of the body. When

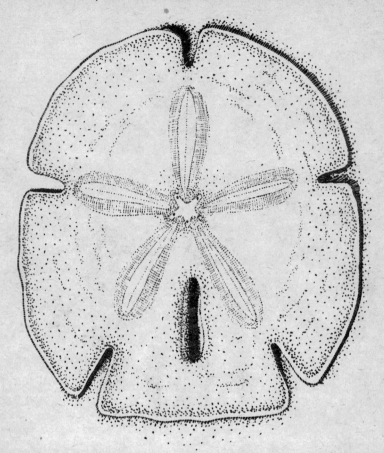

Fig 25   The sand-dollar is closely related to the sea-urchin but is only the thickness of a biscuit. They are found on sandy shores in many parts of the world, but they easily become broken up into segments. This specimen is 4in across

alive, the body is covered with spines which are all backwardly directed and the mouth is protected by a bony plate. These are adaptions to their feeding habit as the heart-urchins burrow in sand or mud and, indeed, spend the whole of their lives passing the sand through the gut and extracting organic material from it. There are five species found around the British coasts, and the

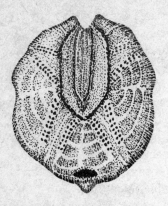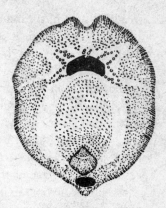

Fig 26   The external skeleton of a heart-urchin is very fragile, but somehow remains intact on the winter coasts of Britain. It is only when human beings tread on them that they are destroyed. On left, view from above. On right, view from below

beachcomber will come across their very fragile and generally white or grey skeletal remains along sandy beaches generally after storms or in the early Spring. They are so fragile that special arrangements will have to be made to transport them. A biscuit tin containing cavities moulded into cellophane will be found to be satisfactory. On 19 April 1971 several dozens of heart-urchins were found along the beaches at Dornock on the coast of Sutherland.

THE SAND-DOLLAR

A number of different sea-urchin species are specially adapted to a sandy shore environment. Whilst some are burrowers such as *Spatangus purpureus* of British coasts, others are found sitting on the surface. The latter are extremely flattened and plate-like and, indeed, have been given the name of sand-dollars. When living they are covered with fine silky spines but the dead skeletal remains found on the shore are practically white with five slots more or less prominent according to species. There is a beautiful pore structure which cannot be appreciated except with a powerful lens. Where there is a strong wave action the sand-dollar breaks up into five, roughly triangular, pieces. On some beaches only the triangular pieces are very evident. On the wonderful 28 mile beach on the north-west coast of the North Island of New Zealand, they are known as snapper biscuits and they are thrown into the sea in the belief that they will cause the snapper fish to be attracted to the bait of the fisherman. So far, I have only found snapper biscuits on the beach. My own sand-dollar specimen was purchased from a flower store specialising in dried flowers and fruits in Lexington Avenue, New York, for – appropriately enough – just a dollar.

The crinoids or sea lilies and feather-stars are members of the starfish group, the *Echinodermata* but they are very much reduced now as members of the world's fauna compared with what they were in Paleozoic times. Not only that, but in those times the crinoids were the dominant forms of the class, the starfish and sea-urchins were relatively rare. Although a number of species are free and able to move about on the ocean floor and indeed some even swim – feather-stars – the crinoids are best known for the long slender stalk which anchors them to a rock or other hard substrate. Both the stalk, cup and tentacle-like rays are seen to be made up of segments similar to little beads. They are usually to be found in deepish water and the beachcomber will only rarely come across them. On the other hand he may come across the feather-stars if they are cast up with masses of seaweed after storms. Fossil crinoids however, can sometimes be found on British beaches, often split up into their small segments. They are to be found by the observant on the sands between Lindisfarne and the mainland of Northumberland at low tide especially after a storm. Here they are known as Cuthbert's beads, and those in my own collection were found, appropriately enough, by a Miss Cuthbertson in 1935.

Chapter 6

Animals with Jointed Legs

In the *Arthropoda*, the great phylum of animals with jointed appendages, there are two main major groups or classes, and a number of smaller ones. The *Insecta*, which are by far the most numerous in species, whilst populating almost every conceivable habitat on land have only a handful of species associated with a marine environment. On the other hand, the *Crustacea* have populated aquatic habitats, most of which are marine, although there are a considerable number of freshwater species. Land species are relatively rare but are very much more common than marine insects.

CRUSTACEA

This is a group of the animal kingdom with which most people are familiar and which, in most people's minds would be associated, rightly, with crabs and lobsters. The group is also associated with the insects, spiders and their relatives, centipedes and millipedes (as well as a few other groups of less familiar creatures), to form one of the main phyla of animals known as the *Arthropoda*. In these animals the head and the anus are at opposite ends of a somewhat elongated body, although in the crabs this is less pronounced. The central nervous system consists of a brain in the dorsal position at the head and a series of linked ganglia along the ventral wall of the body. Perhaps the most important character, however, is the presence of a pair of appendages arising from each segment of the body. These appendages are jointed and each segment is movable. Usually there is considerable specialisation amongst the appendages arising from the various segments.
The arthropods are divided into five distinct classes, the first of which is:

Class 1   *Crustacea;* these include the crabs, crayfish, lobsters, shrimps, wood-lice, slaters, barnacles and water-fleas. These groups are very dissimilar in appearance but their distinctive features are described later. The first three named, as well as the barnacles, are of interest to the beachcomber.

Class 2   *Onychophora;* this class consists only of the curious *Peripatus* which is caterpillar-like and usually found amongst rotting wood. They are sometimes called velvet worms from their appearance. They are rare and of no interest to the beachcomber.

Class 3   *Myriapoda* contains the millipedes and centipedes of which there are no marine examples.

Class 4   *Insecta;* this most important class of animal is normally terrestrial or of fresh water but, although there are almost no marine species, they are often to be found on beaches. This is due to their great mobility, due to flight. Insects are sometimes washed up onto the shore after they have flown out onto the sea during an unsuccessful migration.

Class 5   *Arachnida* consists of the spiders, scorpions and mites of which there are no marine species, if one excepts the peculiar spider-like pycno-gonids, and are unlikely to be of interest to the beachcomber.

THE DECAPODS

The crabs, lobsters, crayfish, prawns and shrimps all belong to this important group of the *Crustacea*. In fact almost all of the largest and most familiar examples of the latter class of the *Arthropoda* are classified as *Decapoda*. The general characters are well known to everyone who has had to handle them as food. The head and thorax together, known as the cephalothorax is covered by a single shield-like skeleton – the carapace. The true crabs, or *Brachyura*, represent the highest development of the *Crustacea* and are characterised by the very broad carapace and the relatively small tail which is tucked forwards under the carapace. Of the five pairs of legs, the first pair are specially modified as claws and they are strong and heavily armoured. The last four pairs are slender and used for walking. Because of the breadth of the carapace many crabs find it easier to walk sideways and, in contrast to the lobsters, crabs usually have small antennae. Some species of spider crabs are the largest *Crustacea* living today, indeed they are

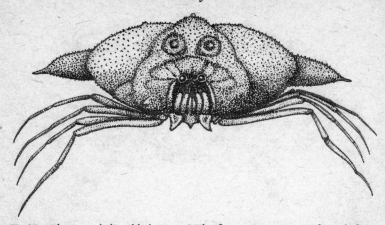

Fig 27   Almost unbelievable but true! The face-on appearance of a crab from Bangkok; over 2in across, it bears a striking resemblance to a fierce face with a pair of large eyes (pink in my dried specimen), a pair of lateral 'horns' and massive teeth! What do they try to scare?

the largest arthropods. They attain a width of 5 or 6ft across the outstretched legs.

Crabs are to be found everywhere – on mud flats, sandy shores, rocky shores, pebbly shores, deep water, sometimes even above the high-tide mark. Many are of bizarre shapes, some are of a fantastic size. Their reproductive rate must be extremely high because often after a storm their lifeless bodies are to be found in great numbers along the beaches. In order to get specimens for one's collection, the beach must be combed *before* the seagulls have had time to carry out *their* combing. After a storm there is much for them to pick over and eat, but the crabs will always be the first delicacy of the day, so speed is essential.

The range of adaptations to differing modes of life in many of the crabs is enormous. The crab from Bangkok which is illustrated, looks like an enormous tick. It is able to bring its eight legs under the shelter of the wing-like expansions of the carapace, and the large horny claw-bearing legs can be brought downwards and fit accurately over the mouth parts and the whole front end of the body. This crab, which is about $2\frac{1}{2}$in in width, then looks remark-

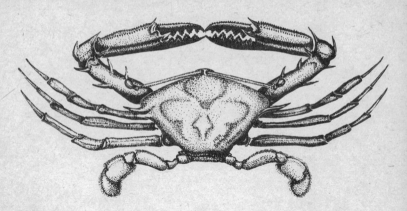

Fig 28   A crab from Bangkok with its eyes set on extremely long stalks. The last pair of legs are modified for swimming

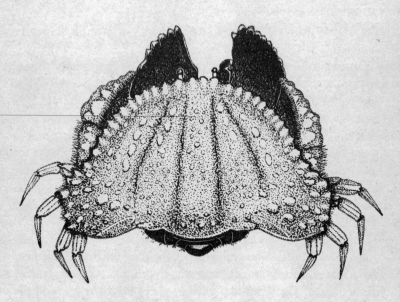

Fig 29   A crab from Bangkok whose greatly enlarged claws can be pulled down over the mouth-parts and thus filter the sand from the water drawn in for respiration. This no doubt confers advantages when predators are on the prowl

ably like a sea-urchin and no doubt this gives protection against some predators.

THE HERMIT CRABS

One of the most highly specialised of adaptations is to be found in the hermit crabs. They are always to be found living in the empty shells of marine gastropods, the whorled single-valved, sea snail shells. The hermit crab's body is modified to an extraordinary degree for living in the shell. In the first place many species have one claw, while in the remaining species both claws are modified to act as an operculum, sealing off the entrance to the shell whorl by fitting it exactly. It thus presents an almost impenetrable barrier to an intruder. In many species only two pairs of walking legs are functional, the hinder two pairs being very much reduced. Two pairs only are required to scuttle around and drag the shell behind. Because it is so well protected from the front, the abdomen is soft and fine and its appendages are absent except for the sixth pair which are modified as a pair of hooks which are used to hang on to the columella of the shell.

The young hermit crab finds an empty shell such as a periwinkle, and installs himself in it. Occasionally he even kills the occupant. Then as he grows larger, so he transfers himself to larger and larger shells. Other fixed animals such as tube-making worms or barnacles or anemones often attach themselves to the shell either just for the ride or in order to share in any meal which the hermit crab may seize and devour.

The horseshoe crabs or king crabs (*Limulus*) are remarkable animals found along the Atlantic coast of North America from Maine to Yucatan. At one time they were exceedingly numerous, literally millions were to be found along a few miles of shore, but today their numbers have decreased. The adult *Limulus* reaches a length of 30in or so, but half of this is taken up by the stiff bristle-like tail. The adult individuals are to be found ploughing through the surface sand in their search for worms. As one of their popular names imply, they are very much horseshoe shaped, at least the

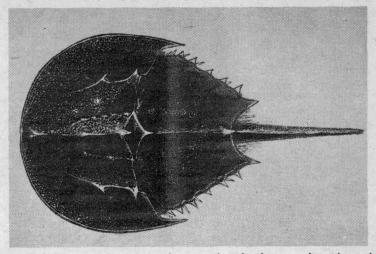

Fig 30   A king-crab, horseshoe crab, or *Limulus*, related more to the spiders and
scorpions than to the crabs. It is found along the Atlantic coast of North America

hood-like forepart. The abdominal segments are joined together
and covered over by a plate-like carapace beset with spines along
the sides. Four of its five pairs of legs are spined and terminated by
pincers and are remarkable in that they function as jaws.

The classification of the *Limulus* is interesting in that it is included
as an order of the *Arachnida* class with the spiders, scorpions, and
mites, but their nearest relatives appear to be the long-extinct
eurypterids, marine, lobster-like animals attaining several feet in
length.

The young of the *Limulus*, however, have a close although
superficial resemblance to a trilobite, another extinct group, but
which are described in Chapter 9.

It often comes as something of a shock to the beachcomber to
learn of the group to which the barnacles belong. He sees them as
fixed, seemingly immobile animals, surrounded by a series of
hard, shell-like scales. Superficially it would appear that they are
related to the molluscs rather than to the *Crustacea*, which is the

Fig 31 Interesting beachcombing can sometimes be done at the fishmongers. This scallop is in various shades of carmine and was included with a number of the common species when a dozen were purchased from the local shop

case. If a living barnacle is observed in an aquarium or a rock pool it is seen to thrust out spasmodically a number of two-branched and segmented appendages. The bristles with which the appendages are fringed collect minute organisms which are then transferred to the mouth and ultimately digested. Another feature connecting the barnacles to the *Crustacea* is the form of the young larva when it hatches from the egg. It possesses three pairs of appendages and swims freely for a time before assuming the immobile adult form. Barnacles may be found on almost any object fixed in the sea, most commonly rocks, but wooden piles and harbour works and the bottoms of ships are well known situations. In addition, barnacles are often found fixed to other animals, some slow moving such as molluscs, but also on the fast moving turtles and even whales.

Wood that has been floating in the sea for any length of time collects a strange assemblage of creatures. The free swimming larvae of the barnacles find it and soon fix onto it where they quickly metamorphose into their typical armour-plated condition, and if the piece of timber comes to rest in a sheltered estuary or lagoon, it can be quickly taken over by a host of mollusc species, especially bivalves which possess an attachment thread or byssus, such as the mussel.

The goosefoot barnacle is quite a prize to find on a piece of timber recently thrown up onto the beach. They are usually in clusters but easily get broken and, I suspect, the seagulls are responsible for this in their never-ending search for anything that looks like food. In searching a beach containing sawn driftwood, the planks should be carefully turned over to see if anything adheres to the underside, but replace them afterwards in case they shelter any living creatures.

Chapter 7

Seashore Shells

Sea shells constitute the most important and certainly the most popular quarry for the beachcomber. A sea shell consists of the hard, generally external but sometimes internal, skeleton secreted by a member of one of the chief divisions of the animal kingdom, the *Mollusca*. This main group is classified to follow the segmented animals with jointed appendages, that is, the insects, spiders, crustaceans, millipedes, centipedes and related groups. The molluscs show no such jointing or segmentation. Of the greatest interest to the beachcomber, however, is the principal type of environment which the molluscs inhabit. Whereas the insects and spiders, almost without exception, are land animals, the molluscs are principally to be found in the sea and in freshwater, but in this habitat they are joined by the crustaceans, the crabs, lobsters and their like.

The beauty of the mollusc shell has stimulated and interested the beach walker over many centuries, while the living contents of the shell, although today a symbol of luxury, used to be one of the chief foods of shore-dwelling peoples.

MOLLUSCA AND CEPHALOPODA

The Mollusca are divided into five distinct groups or classes and the beachcomber will find shells of species of four of these groups, and with some luck, should find some of the fifth group. The five classes are as follows:

1 Molluscs with bivalved shells such as the clams, mussels, cockles and oysters. This class is known as the *pelecypoda*, one of the most important groups for the beachcomber.
2 Molluscs known as the *Amphineura*, the best known of which are the chitons. These are limpet-like, but the shell consists of eight shield-like pieces arranged in a longitudinal band.

63

3 Molluscs with a one-valved shell known as the *Gastropoda*. This class consists of the periwinkles, whelks, cone-shells, cowries, limpets, and many
   others including also the land-snails and the shell-less slugs. This is another
   important group for the beachcomber.
4 Molluscs known as the elephant's-tusk shells or *Scaphopoda*. The shells are
   curved tubes open at both ends but wider at the end corresponding to the
   mouth of the animal. They are sand burrowers and only three genera are
   known. They are not likely to feature widely in the collections of the
   beachcomber.
5 This group is known as the *Cephalopoda* and includes the cuttlefish, squids,
   octopods and nautili. They are more usually referred to as cephalopods
   rather than molluscs, as they are very distinct from the previous four classes.
   All are marine animals with a more highly specialised organisation (including a well-defined head) than is present in the molluscs. A shell is not always
   present in this group but the plate-like internal shell of the cuttlefish is often
   in extraordinary abundance on many shores. In the nautili the shell is often
   chambered, but externally takes a more conventional form.

BIVALVE MOLLUSCS – PELECYPODA

The pelecypods or bivalve molluscs consist of about 10,000 species
and constitute the second largest class. One third of these are freshwater forms, the remainder being marine whilst terrestrial species
are rare. The pelecypods are characterised by the possession of two
shells or 'valves' hinged together by a horny ligament, by a distinct
head being absent and by the absence also of a toothed tongue or
radula.

The food usually consists of minute plant life drawn in to the
animal through a tubular siphon. A second siphon expels the
water and waste products. Oxygen is taken in by the same
method.

SCALLOPS

Amongst the most well known of all bivalve molluscs are the
scallops, the common name given to the several hundred species
of the family *Pectinidae*. A number of species are fairly large and
are relished as food in many parts of the northern hemisphere. They

Fig 32   The large, pink barnacles, *Balanus decorus*, on the knobbed whelk, *Austrofusus glans*. New Zealand; 3in long

are related to the oysters but unlike the latter which are fixed, the scallops are able to swim freely at least to a limited extent, by flapping the two valves together.

PEN OR FAN SHELLS

On the British coasts only one species of the family *Pinnidae* occurs. These are the pen or fan shells and the British species is the fan mussel, *Pinna fragilis*. This is the largest of British shells and it sometimes reaches a length of 15in, and a width of 8in. The giant Mediterranean pen, *Pinna nobilis*, grows to something like the same size. The specimen illustrated was collected in Lipari. It has a number of white tubercles on the reddish-orange shell, especially on the curved margin. The golden byssus threads of the giant Mediterranean pen were collected by the ancients to form a fleece.

SOLENIDAE

The long tubular shells of the mollusc known variously as the razorfish, spoutfish, or (in America) jack-knife clam are a characteristic of many sandy beaches, and in Britain alone there are seven species classified in the family *Solenidae*, all of which are sand burrowers. The two valves form a long tube each of which is reminiscent of the old 'cut-throat' razor. Some species are quite large, *Ensis arcuatus* being up to 150mm long. At West Wittering in Sussex, the species *Solen marginatus* is especially abundant. It is identified from other species by the transverse groove around the anterior, 'hinged', end (as though it had been tied with string when soft). When the skin is adhering to the valves, the colour is pale yellow or orange, but when they have been washed onto the beach they are often black and white and show the delicate way in which the layers of shell have been deposited. As with all bivalves, when collected they should be tied together with thread so that the two valves are always associated.

One may have to discard a number of shells before a perfect hinged pair is found.

THE TEREDO SHIPWORM

Other animals make their home actually inside floating or submerged wood. The classic species is, of course, the shipworm or *Teredo* which has plagued those that have sailed in wooden hulled ships since time immemorial. Even today, those that sail the hulls of timber must take care of this pestilent wood-destroyer. Perhaps today, although the dhows that ply the Indian Ocean are riddled with these pests, the greatest hazard is to harbour works and other submerged timber that does not necessarily sail the oceans. Although the *Teredo* is called a shipworm, it is indeed a bivalve mollusc just as is an oyster or a mussel. The shell valves are however, very small, usually not much more than a quarter of an inch across. The body of the shipworm, on the other hand, although normally about 10-12in long may grow to as much as

Fig 33 The precious wentletrap has an alabaster-like appearance. The specimen illustrated is from Queensland, an area of the world little known at the time when the Chinese thought so highly of them

3ft. The borings in the timber are characteristic. For one thing the tunnels are lined with a thick coating of chalk which no wood-boring insect shows. Then, again, the external aperture, that is to the sea water, is very small, just of a size for the siphons of the mollusc to obtrude in order to inhale and exhale the sea water. For many years there has existed controversy as to whether the *Teredo* obtains nutrients from the wood substance, but I think this has now been proved beyond doubt, although food is augmented from the digestion of minute organisms introduced by the inhalant siphon.

OYSTERS

The 'true' oysters of Europe belong to the genus *Ostrea*, the British native being *O. edulis*. Unfortunately, due to over-fishing, it has disappeared from many estuaries and even in situations where it was still holding on disease has brought stocks to a very low level. For many years, however, it has been the practice to import immature oysters and to 'plant' them in favourable situations in British estuaries and fatten them for market. Before the war the American blue-point oyster *Ostrea virginica* was imported for fattening, and also brought with it were two important oyster pests, the slipper limpet, *Crepidula fornicata* and the American

67

Fig 34   The large and heavy toha roha shells are found in a few of the long sandy beaches in the North Island of New Zealand. The large muscular foot with which the bivalve buries itself in the sand is a great delicacy. It is, however, highly protected by law, the 'open season' extending only to a few days and the number which can be collected by any one person is limited

whelk tingle species *Urosalpinx cinerea*. Another imported species is the Portuguese oyster, *Ostrea angulata*, which is not so flat as the British native. It rarely breeds in British waters.

The wing oysters, *Pteriidae*, are mostly tropical and some are large, *Pteria penguin*, the giant wing oyster being 7in in length. The base of the shell, at the hinge, is extended into beak-like projections. The beachcomber must be very careful in handling these shells as the beaks break easily. The pearl oysters consist of six tropical species of the genus *Margaritifera* (sometimes called *Pinctado*). The black-lipped oyster *M. margaritifera*, produces the most pearls but the smaller Japanese pearl oyster, *M. mertensi*, is also fished extensively. The so-called thorny oysters are rather like scallops in shape. Indeed they are more closely related to these bivalves than to the true oysters! The thorny oysters, *Spondylidae*, possess long, spatulate spines and are often richly coloured. Although relatively abundant they mostly occur in tropical deep water. The saddle oysters, *Anomiidae*, otherwise known as jingle-shells, have a flat thin fragile lower valve in which there is a pear-shaped opening. This is the site of the attachment to a base, usually an old shell, and made by means of a calcareous plug. There are four British species.

CLAMS

Clam is the name given to a number of families of bivalves where the two valves are similar in size and shape and 'clamped' together. Perhaps the best known is the giant clam, *Tridacna gigas*, of the Indo-Pacific coral reefs, which may be from 2 to 4ft in length. The two valves are convoluted. The Atlantic surf clam of North America is found on sandy beaches and is the source of clam chowder. The oblong surf clam, *Lutraria oblonga*, is found on similar shores in Western Europe and is up to 5in in length. The tellins are tropical, sand-dwelling clams with highly polished valves of paper thinness. The sunrise tellin, *Tellina radiata*, is common in the West Indies and the Bahamas, and is used together with other species in the manufacture of shell jewelry and shell craft. A European species is *Tellina tenius* – about 1in in length. The Venus clams (*Veneridae*) consist of about 400 world-wide species. The hinges possess interlocking teeth. Often the shells are ridged and sometimes bear long spines.

Except for the giant South African wedge clam, *Donax serva*, which may be up to 3in in length, the wedge clams are relatively small. There are about 50 species distributed almost throughout the world on sandy beaches. They are often delicately coloured. The lucine clams are tropical in distribution, have round shells and the anterior muscle scar on the shell is long and narrow.

COCKLES

Cockles, *Cardiidae*, are well known for providing human food.

Some species, for example the common cockle, *Cardium edule*, are often present in prodigious quantities. It has been estimated that in a cockle-bed in South Wales well over a million cockles are present per acre, and there are 320 acres! The edible cockle is about an inch in length with a chalky-white shell. The shell is covered with spine-like projections with which it can grip the sand in which it lives and through which it can move with surprising speed by means of its muscular 'foot'. Other species of cockle have different sorts of projections for sand-gripping, such as ridges or plate-like spines. There are eleven British species of cockle, the largest of which may be up to 4in long. The spiny cockle, *Cardium aculeatum*, is a good example. It is found on the South Devon coast and the Channel Islands.

MUSSELS

Mussels are said to be the most abundant of all molluscs. Their long, acute-angled valves must be familiar to everyone. They are often dark blue in colour as is the edible mussel, *Mytilus edulis*. They occur throughout the rocky shores of Europe and north-east America. The colonies are so dense that it is often difficult to conceive that another individual could possibly be accommodated. When very dry, the blue colour often peels off as a horny layer. The New Zealand species is bright green in colour.

THE CHITONS

The chitons or coat-of-mail shells are now usually classified in a separate class of the molluscs known as the *Loricata*. They are exceptionally easy to identify as they all possess eight overlapping shell-like plates which lie along the back. Surrounding these plates is a horny or fleshy girdle by means of which the chiton adheres to the rock on which it lives much in the manner of a limpet. Although when living the chiton is flat or slightly arched, when it becomes separated from its substrate it curls up to a greater or lesser extent and is more likely to be found in this condition. In

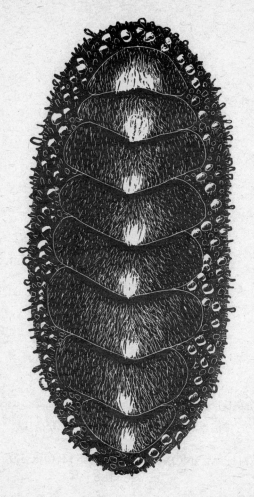

Fig 35 *Chiton echinata* from Chile is nearly 5in long. The plates are mauve-purple and the surrounding girdle is beset with white bulbous papillae

Britain, there are two main groups of chitons, four species in the *Lepidopleurida* being found beyond low-water mark whilst the eight species in the *Chitonida* are to be found between tides.

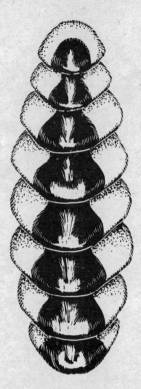

Fig 36 The mail-shell, *Katerina tunicata* from California is about 3in in length. The sides of the shell valves have the appearance of alabaster. It seems to have lost its girdle

THE MONOVALVES—GASTROPODA
CONCHES

Almost everyone will be familiar with the large showy shells known as conches. These are the shells of molluscs classified in the family *Strombidae* and there are about 80 species, all from the warm water of the tropics and sub-tropics. One of the best known is the queen conch from the West Indies. It grows to about 12in and is common enough to be an important article of diet in the Bahamas and many other areas.

The various species of conch however have become so widely

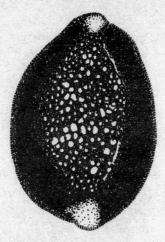

Fig 37   The snakeshead cowrie, *Cypraea caputserpentis*, is so called because of its scaly appearance and shape. It is a common species of the Indo-Pacific region

collected and used almost as articles of commerce in local souvenir shops that the beachcomber will almost certainly have to comb these shops for his specimens. Those that have been used as food can be identified by a cut in the shell.

The spider conches are ten species in the same family which are characterised by a number of finger-like prolongations of the shell mouth. They are all Indo-Pacific in distribution but again they are widely collected by local dealers for sale in souvenir and floral décor shops, and almost certainly this is only where the itinerant beachcomber will find them.

The giant spider conch *Lambis truncata* is a common inhabitant of many areas of the Indian Ocean and can be anything up to 12in long. It is bluey-grey in colour with almost black projections.

COWRIES

It is hard to define why the finding of a cowrie shell gives so much pleasure. It is certainly not because the cowrie was used as money by native peoples living in tropical areas, nor because it was used as a religious symbol and an important ornament. Perhaps it is because the glossy, porcelain-like appearance of the shell is especially attractive being rounded and full with two long, usually, fluted lips. The 160 or so different species are variously patterned and coloured with spots. A few have the appearance of gemstones; one is called the carrelian cowrie and another the onyx cowrie. Whereas many are very common, especially along tropical shores, others are exceedingly rare, such as the golden cowrie, *Cypraea aurantium*, from Melanesia.

Generally, cowries are approximately an inch in length, but some species are about 4in. Cowrie shells of different species are often to be seen for sale in souvenir shops in many towns and cities of the world, especially on the coast.

ROYAL TYRIAN PURPLE

A murex from the Mediterranean, the dye murex or *Murex brandaris*, was the origin of considerable commerce amongst the early civilisations in this area. The Phoenicians found that they could obtain a good rich purple dye from the yellow secretion of this mollusc which was suitable for both wool and cotton. It commanded a great prize and, indeed, during the time of the Romans 'purple' was worn exclusively by the emperors and senators. In the early Christian church purple was incorporated into the robes of cardinals and since then this colour has often been used for the robes of dignitaries and others, of high academic rank. It has been stated that many new towns were sited and settled in the western Mediterranean by the Phoenicians when they had found new areas where the dye murex could be found and exploited.

WENTLETRAPS

The 200 or so species in the family *Epitoniidae* of the molluscs are generally known as wentletraps. So far, the origin or meaning of this curious word has eluded me. The shells are characterised by the rather loose whorls being encircled by a series of white or light coloured ridges. Many wentletraps are white or almost so and often possess a curious appearance similar to alabaster. The precious wentletrap, *Epitonium scalare*, from Eastern Asia was at one time an object of great rarity and used as an ornament. There are five species around British coasts although they are mostly uncommon. Most wentletraps, when alive, are associated with sea anemones or corals and they excrete a purple substance. One of the largest is the magnificent wentletrap, *Amaea magnifica*, a 4in long species from Japanese waters.

THE WORM SHELLS

The first six or so whorls of this shell follows the normal 'snail' pattern then afterwards the whorl develops erratically and the tight whorling is lost. It then takes on the appearance of the tube of one of the marine worms, hence the name given to these curious shells. They are not to be found around the British coasts, but a number of species occur along the southern part of the east coast of the USA into the Gulf of Mexico and the Caribbean region. The slit worm shell grows up to 6in long, is found around the West Indian islands and Florida, and in this species even the first whorls of the shell are erratic.

LIMPETS

The limpets or true limpets consist of about 400 species to be found on the rocks of shores of most of the temperate countries of the world. They are classified in the family *Acmaeidae* although this family now appears to have been subdivided. They are generally pyramidal in shape although the outer margin of some species is sometimes extended into rays. In life they fit closely onto the rock and are held well-nigh immovable by means of a strong muscular foot. Around the British coasts there are nine true limpets of which the common limpet, *Patella vulgata*, is extremely abundant. It occasionally reaches a length of nearly 3in. Some species, however, are very small. The blue-rayed limpet, *Patina*

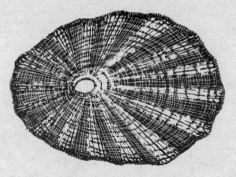

Fig 38   Some of the keyhole limpets, as shown in this species, *Fissurella maxima*, from Puget Sound, show an attractive pattern of radiating stripes. The hole in the shell is used for excretion

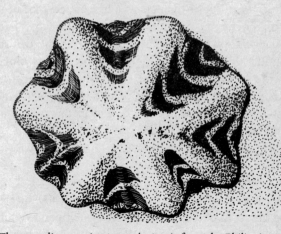

Fig 39   The sweet limpet, *Acmaea saccharina*, is from the Philippines, but is also to be found throughout the Indo-Pacific region

pellucida, is exceptional in not living on rock but on the fronds of oar-weed. The shell is golden-brown with a series of blue lines radiating from the apex. The colour of the 'head-scar' inside the shell in the apex is of great importance in identifying the various British species.

The keyhole limpets constitute a family of several hundred species known as the *Fissurellidae*. They are found mostly in the warm water of the tropics and sub-tropics, and they are characterised by the possession of a hole at the apex of the otherwise typical pyramidal limpet shell. The largest species, the giant keyhole limpet, *Megathura crenulata*, is found between the tides in California and reaches a length of 5in. Another large species is the maximum keyhole limpet, *Fissurella maxima*, from the intertidal zone of the Chile coast and it reaches a length of 3in. Closely related to the keyhole limpets is the Roman shield limpet; its shape is characteristic but it does not possess a keyhole. It is found along the coasts of Australia and only reaches a length of 2in.

The American slipper-limpet, *Crepidula fornicata*, occurs in great profusion at West Wittering in Sussex. Yet this curiously shaped member of the family *Calyptraeidae* was unknown in British waters until about 1890 when it was thought to have been introduced with the blue-point oyster, *Ostrea virginica*, from North America. It is an undesirable inhabitant of the oyster beds as it competes with the latter for food. They are somewhat flattened with a single half-whorl turning to the right, but the character by means of which it is most easily recognised is the glistening white half-floor or 'half-deck' inside. The shells are often a pale fleshy colour, and they attach themselves to any convenient object, often other molluscs, and in some areas more usually they stick onto the backs of their own species, hence their indelicate name *fornicata*. Each shell fits exactly onto the shell of the lower member but when the molluscs die, they become separated and where they are common the beach sometimes consists entirely of their shells. The strangest thing about this species is their sex relationship to their position in the colony or chain. The oldest, lowermost, are female. Then come one or two of intermediate sex, and then the youngest, uppermost, are males. They change sex from male to female with age. In this way curious hardshaped aggregations are formed in whorls consisting of ten or more individuals and a smooth stone may bear a number of such whorls with the small limpets scattered overall. It is to be found on many south and

Fig 40 The slipper limpet, *Crepidula fornicata*, is a North American species which was introduced into England with oysters round about 1890. Today some beaches along the English south coast are made up entirely of their shells. *Above*, two clusters of the limpets clinging to each other; *below*, a limpet from beneath, showing the characteristic 'half-deck'

eastern shores in England. There is only one native British species in the family called the Chinaman's hat, *Calyptraea chinensis*.

TUSK SHELLS—SCAPHOPODA

The tusk shells, or rather the scaphopods, burrow in the sand with the smaller or sharper end of the tusk protruding. They live on minute animals and usually large numbers of the tusk shells are

Fig 41   *Acanthina brevi-dentata* from Mawe, Panama. Length: 1in

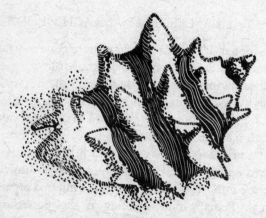

Fig 42   *Thais mancinella*, a member of the *Muricidae* from the Philippines. About
$1\frac{1}{2}$in long

found together. There are five British species of which one,
Dentalium vulgare, is to be found in the south-west and South
Wales, whereas *Dentalium entalis* is frequent in the north and
scarce in the south. The other three species are found in the Shetlands and extreme north of Scotland, although south-west Ireland
is a good location to look for a number of species.

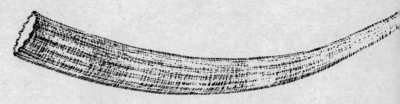

Fig 43   The elephant-tusk shell, *Dentalium elephantum*, from the Philippines, is white tinged with green. It is open at both ends and the specimen is 4½in long

My specimen of *Dentalium elephantum* from the Philippines bears ten longitudinal ridges and except for the pointed end is green, giving it a resemblance to a small stick of celery.

THE LAMP SHELLS—BRACHIOPODA

The 'arm-footed' animals or *Brachiopoda* are relatively rare animals today, and there are only about 200 known living species, very local in distribution. But at other times in the history of life on earth, they were exceedingly common and over 3,000 species are known as fossils. They have been of enormous value in the interpretation of the age of the various geological formations. At first sight a brachiopod looks very much like a bivalve mollusc, having two opposed shells whose outer rims fit into each other, but there are important differences in the internal organisation of the animal. Perhaps most striking is the possession by the brachiopod of a pair of spirally coiled tentacles or arms. The correct name of this structure is the lophophore similar to the organ found in the *Bryozoa* but not found in molluscs. Another important difference between brachiopods and bivalve molluscs is that whilst in the latter the shells occupy the 'sides' of the animal, in brachiopods the two shells occupy the top and bottom positions of the animal. In addition there is a stalk by means of which the brachiopod anchors itself to some substrate such as a rock. In one genus, however, *Lingula*, the burrowing habit is found and the stalk is very long, several times the length of the shells and serves to pull the animal up and down its vertical burrow. Incidentally, the genus *Lingula* is thought to hold the record as being the oldest genus of animals still alive on the earth today. Brachiopods classified in the genus *Lingula* are thought to have lived 500 million years ago as evidenced from their fossils.

Chapter 8

Cephalopoda -
The Head-Footed Animals

The cephalopods are the most highly developed of the molluscs and in this animal class belong the octopus, squid, argonauts and nautilus. The class-name refers to the tentacles, of which there may be eight, ten or many more which surround the head. Throughout the group there is a progressive loss of shell. In the octopus a shell is absent, whilst in the squids and cuttlefish it is internal, but when the animal dies the cuttlefish bone (as it is called) is eventually cast upon the shore. It is shaped like a spearhead, white and chalky, being usually round and about 6in in length. One species found in New Zealand bears a sooty streak. The giant squid of the north Atlantic can grow up to 50ft long, and is the largest of all invertebrates. The sperm whales feed on this species when it is about 5 or 6ft long, at great ocean depths, and their horny beaks are often recovered from the whales' stomachs. Cuttlefish are rather robust looking and thick, whilst squids are more elongated with a triangular tail-fin.

The eyes of the octopus and those of squid and cuttlefish are the most highly developed of all invertebrates, and indeed approach the complexity of those of man.

NAUTILUS AND ARGONAUT

Very different in superficial appearance to the other cephalopods are the three species of nautilus which differ from all the other members of the group by the possession of an external, coiled shell. It protects itself by retiring into the shell and covering the opening with a thick, warty skin in the manner of an operculum of the more primitive molluscs. The shell is divided into a number

82

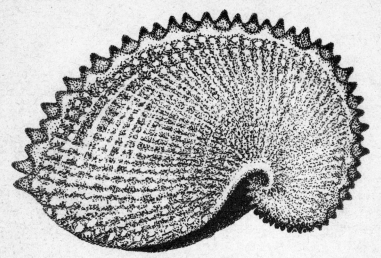

Fig 44   The very fragile paper nautilus is actually an egg case secreted only by the female. New Zealand

of chambers, but the body of the nautilus is accommodated only in the outer, largest one.

The pearly nautilus, *Nautilus pompilius*, grows to about 8in across. It is found on the muddy bottom of deep water in the western Pacific. The female nautilus has a narrower lodgment chamber than has the male. The shell has a number of brown, transverse, zebra-like markings, and is seldom found except when specially sought.

The common paper nautilus, *Argonauta argo*, reaches a length of 12in, whilst the nodosa paper nautilus, *Argonauta nodosa*, may measure 5in, and the brown paper nautilus, *Argonauta hians*, has a maximum length of 3in. All these species are found only in warm, tropical seas, although the 'shells' may be carried great distances, ultimately reaching shores far from the regions of the ocean where the animal lived. The shells are sometimes found in antique shops, with the shell carved and decorated showing the pearly layer.

The argonauts are closely related to the octopus group, and indeed

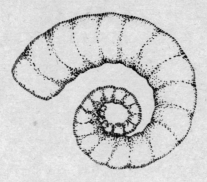

Fig 45   The small white chambered shell of the decapod squid *Spirula spirula* found on the shores of warm seas of many parts of the world and occasionally on the British shores. This specimen is from the Bahamas and measures nearly 1in

Fig 46   The shell of the *spirula* squid is shown half-protruding from its body. In contrast to its shell the squid is rarely found by marine biologists. The total length with arms extended is about 8in. Drawn from a model in the American Museum of Natural History, New York

the male bears a strong resemblance. The female, however, secretes a fine paper-thin shell in which the eggs are deposited. These shells are extremely delicate and fragile and it is a source of amazement that they finally reach the shore without damage.

SPIRULA

Spirula shells are found in various parts of the world rather locally, but sometimes in great profusion. They have been found by the writer on two sandy shores, one in the North Island of New Zealand, and the other on the coral sands of Harbour Island in the

Bahamas. They are unlike any other shell being tubular and spiral, but the turns are not in contact. They are completely chambered by a series of concave septa each of which is pierced by a continuous tube called the siphuncle. Without any knowledge of the animal that produces it, one is tempted to ask 'where in the shell does the animal dwell?' However, the shell protrudes slightly from the back of a squid-like decapod and appears to have no function. The living *Spirula* is flesh-coloured with an arrow-shaped body and a globular head bearing eight small tentacles and two long ones. It is collected only rarely by the marine biologist, my own drawing being made from a model in the American Museum of Natural History, New York.

The shells of the tropical species *Spirula peronii* are occasionally found on British beaches.

Chapter 9

Combing
the Beaches of the Past

A considerable proportion of the present dry land of the world was once – or more than once – under the sea. These seas were inhabited by the sea creatures which had evolved at the various ages of the past. The impressions made by them in the rocks and their mineralised skeletal parts are known as 'fossils' so that when we collect them, we are combing the beaches of the past! Many of these animal species whose remains we can find in the rocks have disappeared during the course of evolution. They are not to be found living today. This is not the place to give anything but the most cursory glance at the fossil history of animals and plants; this is an immense subject and information is best sought from more specialised books, but there is one interesting point which we should keep in mind. Many beaches are points of erosion where wave action is wearing down and breaking up rock structures. These latter often represent old beaches with their complement of fossils. These get washed out so that many of our present-day beaches are strewn with the fossilised animal remains of beaches of the past. Often they may mislead us into thinking that they are modern.

The piece of shoreline stretching from Bognor in Sussex to Barton in Hampshire, must be one of the most remarkable beachcombing areas in the world. There is a rich molluscan fauna living in and on the extensive sands that lie inshore to the Isle of Wight. In addition, there are here and there beds of clay and soft-stone in which several species of bivalve mollusc bore, moreover much marine life of other classes is represented. But the amazing phenomenon of fossil shells of a number of species lying in the sand alongside modern species is quite extraordinary. The fossil-

Fig 47   A fossil solitary coral of the Devonian period. Length: 4in

bearing rocks have been washed by the sea, and the fossils themselves must be rather harder than the rocky matrix because the
fossils get washed out often in good condition. It is interesting to
contemplate that when they become embedded in the sand and
mud, they will eventually become consolidated into stone again,
although these fossils will give no indication of the age of its
formation. They will, however, give information of the time of
the breakdown of their basic stone formation and the new fossils,
those animals at present constituting the present living fauna, will
date the new presently forming strata.

The fossils we find at Wittering are derived from what are known
as the Bracklesham beds. These were laid down in the Lower
Eocene period, more particularly during the Cuisian times. This
was something in the region of 50 million years ago, yet many of
the fossils we pick up on the sand we could quite easily take for
the shells of present day animals. Pieces of turret shell are common,
but it is difficult to find specimens with the top of the spire intact.
The nearest thing to my own specimens in the British Museum's
British Caenozoic Fossils is the species *Turritella sulcifera*.

There is also a strange fossil oyster which has a strongly ridged
shell; if viewed from the top, this curls around to the right. My
specimens, found near to East Head at West Wittering, are more
slender and curl more strongly (or appear to because of their slim

Fig 48   The beachcomber should develop his powers of observation under all circumstances. The fossil bivalve mollusc (*right*), was found in some road-mending material containing blast-furnace clinker. The specimen had been through the blast-furnace but still retained its shape. *Left*, fossil heart-urchins

profile) than the species *Ostrea plicata* figured in the publication named above. It is rather difficult to find a new species of shell-bearing mollusc today, yet it is not so very difficult to collect a species of Eocene mollusc not previously described. A Saturday afternoon stroll through the sand can sometimes produce very gratifying results!

Essential books of reference for the beachcomber around British shores of the past as well as around many of our present ones, are the paperback handbooks of the British Museum (Natural History), *British Caenozoic Fossils* (*Tertiary* and *Quaternary*) mentioned earlier. First published 1960. It contains 44 pages of excellent line drawings with much information of great interest including lists of fossil species that can be found in various localities. Also recommended are *British Mesozoic Fossils* (first published 1962) and *British Palaeozoic Fossils*, first published in 1964. The latter contains 69 pages of line drawings of fossils. Altogether these three publications are a valuable source of information, and are designed to help in the identification of fossils found in Britain by providing sets of accurate drawings of the typical species found in the classical sites at the various horizons. Although paperback, they are beautiful book productions and are excellent value at 30p, 62½p and 65p respectively.

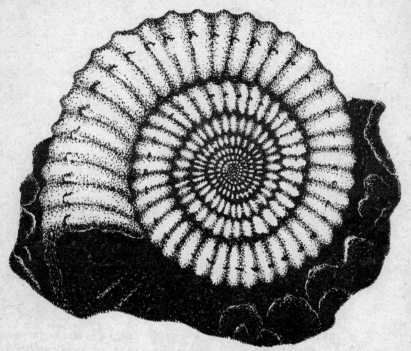

Fig 49   The ammonites which are now extinct were very abundant in Mesozoic times. The 'shell' consisted of a large number of separate chambers but connected by a tube. In some respects a resemblance to the nautilus is shown. Charmouth on the Dorset coast was the best known collecting locality but they are now protected

With these books, having found some fossil material, the beach-comber can carry out the identification himself thereby exercising his critical faculties. The beachcomber should measure his ability to observe natural objects in their own natural setting with his ability to match his specimen with descriptive text, or an illustration in a book.

TRILOBITES

Of all the animals that the beachcomber can find when he

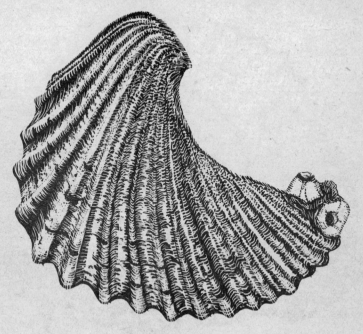

Fig 50 The fossil oyster, *Ostrea plicata*, with a right-handed wing-like extension is washed out of the Bracklesham beds on the Sussex coast. It could be taken for a recent shell on the sandy shore and two barnacles have attached themselves.

searches the beaches of the past, those that have fascinated the writer most have been the *Trilobites*. These marine animals (they are only found in association with marine deposits) were of the greatest importance in Paleozoic times. The trilobites constitute a separate class of the *Arthropoda* but they are unique in the respect that no living examples now exist. They were of the greatest importance in the Cambrian system attaining the peak of their development in the Ordovician period. They then declined, markedly in the Devonian, until in the Carboniferous a few only survived. These latter were small in size and only a few genera were represented. None survived the Carboniferous period in Europe, although one species of Permian age has been found in America. In size, trilobites were generally about a couple of

Fig 51 The trilobite, *Ampyx nudis*. An ancestor of present day arthropods

inches in length but they varied from only a quarter of an inch (*Agnostus*) to over 10in, indeed examples are known of up to 20in (*Paradoxides*).

The head is covered by a semicircular shield-like carapace, but the feature which has given the name to the group concerns the body which is distinctly divided into a median axial lobe and two lateral lobes on each of the many segments. The Philosophical Transactions for 1698 make interesting reading. In it is contained one of the earliest references to trilobites. This is in a communication by the curator of the Ashmolean Museum in Oxford, Edward Lloyd by name. He referred to his specimens from Llandeilo in South Wales but he thought they were the 'Sceleton of a Flat Fish'. In the following year, however, he published two illustrations from which the species he mentioned can be identified.

SUBMERGED FORESTS

The beachcomber also will sometimes find himself combing the land of the past when, at low water, he finds the old water-worn stumps of trees. This is when the coastline is sinking and the sea has invaded the forest. These submerged forests are numerous around the British Isles and perhaps are best known on the East Anglian coast, as well as along the shores of Lincolnshire, West Cornwall, Cheshire and the Gower Peninsula. But there are many more besides and their presence is often indicated in local guide books. Neolithic stone axes have been associated with submerged forests, and it was thought at one time that all of the latter were of Neolithic age, but the indications are that this is not so. The remains of the forest trees are firmly locked into the shore. The soil has usually been removed and often replaced by sand, but the roots are held fast by the underlying rocky strata, remaining thus for several thousand years. Submergence in salt water has effectively prevented the action of woodrotting fungi and wood-boring insects, but the softer bark and sapwood have usually been removed by wave action.

Chapter 10

Fish

Fish constitute a major class of animals and they are especially adapted to a life in fresh and salt water. The skin surface, in spite of generally being scaled, is smooth and offers little resistance to motion through the water, while their shape is the result of evolution on hydrodynamic principles.

The fins of a fish are of two main kinds. Firstly, the paired fins of which there are two, correspond to the limbs of vertebrates which live on land. The pectoral fins correspond to the fore-limbs and the pelvic to the hind-limbs. Secondly, there are the median fins of which one or more occupy a position in the middle line of the back, these being known as the *dorsals*, the *anal* is situated immediately behind the vent on the underside of the fish and the *caudal* fin is situated around the tail.

A fish obtains the oxygen it requires through the mouth and passing it over a series of thin walled gills in which the blood vessels are highly ramified. The water then passes out. The gills are covered by protective devices for these important, but very delicate organs and these are known as the gill covers. The eyes are often a prominent feature of a fish.

When the bodies of most fish get washed upon the shore, the flesh decomposes unless it is found by a gull or other carrion-eater. The fish that rely on their speed to catch their prey are relatively unprotected by scales so that their remains for the beachcomber are uncommon. The same can be said of those that possess a shape and colour pattern that allows them to lie on the sea bottom undetected, such as the flat fish and the carpet shark. But a comparatively small number of fish are heavily protected from the attentions of predaceous fish and other animals by the provision of large horny or boney scales or spines. These fish are protected even when they are dead and their dried bodies have been collected for centuries and are to be found in the antique and the tourist souvenir shops.

PORCUPINE AND PUFFER FISH

It would be a lucky beachcomber who found a porcupine fish on the shore, although their dried globe-like and prickly bodies are to be found in souvenir shops in a number of parts of the tropical world. These fish are classified in two families, the globe-fish or puffers in the *Tetraodontidae* and the porcupine-fish in the *Diodontidae*. They all possess short, rather globular bodies covered to a greater or lesser extent by spines or prickles. They are thus protected to a degree from predation but this can be considerably increased by the remarkable phenomenon whereby the fish swallows air or water and inflates itself like a spine-covered balloon. The spines stick out at right angles making the fish exceedingly difficult for anyone to handle let alone for a predator to try and bite!

The inflated porcupine-fish float about with the currents generally upside down, and sailors would obtain these and dry them to bring home as souvenirs, the bizarre nature of their possession apparently outweighing the discomfort associated with their packing and transport. Those that one sees for sale nowadays appear to be small and heavily varnished, but the pair which I bought in a junk shop many years ago are large and unvarnished, the outer appearance being rather like parchment.

Sharks are relatively common creatures in most seas of the world and their large size and ferocious habit of preying upon most large animals in the sea including man (when he is to be found there), have earned them a healthy respect. The big jaws furnished with razor-sharp triangular teeth can gape into almost a complete circle, and these have been popular objects of decoration for very many years. Usually they are to be found in the fashionable fish restaurants in the ports of many countries, so that today they have disappeared from the antique shops where, at one time, they were to be found in plenty.

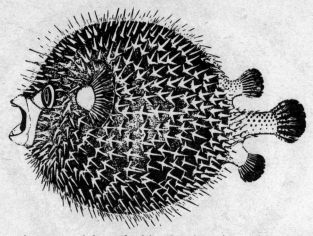

Fig 52   When menaced the puffer-fish inflate themselves with air and this has the effect of causing the spines to stand out. The puffer then floats along with the currents on the sea's surface. They were formerly used as helmets by South Sea islanders and the Chinese used to make lanterns of them. The specimen illustrated is 18in in length and came from a junk shop

Sharks seldom receive much sympathy from the human race, and (unfortunately they share this with all fish) are subject to world-wide attention from 'sporting' fishermen wherever they are to be found in numbers. Elaborate and expensive tackle is employed, as well as the use of specifically designed powerboats. One is more likely to find a pair of shark jaws in the vicinity of an operating fishing centre than along an isolated coastline. Although a number of the jaws are taken by the fishermen as trophies, many are thrown away when once the excitement of the catch has evaporated. The cleaning of a large pair of jaws is a messy business and conventionally the jaws are pulled open until they are both in one plane. When dry the adherent tissue locks them in this position.

When examining the jaws of a shark notice especially the teeth. It will be seen that there are a number of rows. The teeth of the first, or outer row, slope upwards in the lower jaw and down-wards in the upper, the other four rows slope inwards at various

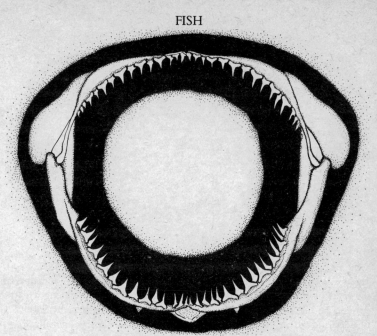

Fig 53   The jaws of sharks dried when in the stretched open position were once common objects to be picked up in the junk shops, but they have now virtually disappeared on account of their use as décor in 'South Sea island' restaurants. The specimen illustrated has an internal gape of 8½in

Fig 54   Teeth of a shark showing the worn functional ones above and the rows of replacement ones below. The latter act as barbs preventing food from slipping forward when once the bite has been taken

Fig 55 The egg-case of a Port Jackson shark, *Heterodontus phillippi*. About 3in in length. Compare with that of the skate and the dogfish. Found in a shell shop in New York

angles until the last row is laying flat with the extremely sharp points protected by a fold of cartilage. Thus, in the shark we see a mechanism whereby the older teeth at the front receive the

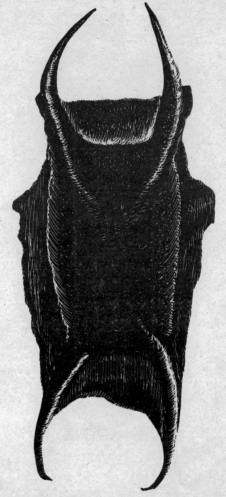

Fig 56   The egg-case of the skate. Total length: 5in; West Wittering, Sussex. The young fish is 'laid' in the case and when fully developed, the case is ruptured and the fish is released

roughest usage, get worn down, and finally are lost. Their place is then taken by newer and younger teeth behind. The shark then, possesses a very efficient apparatus for catching its prey and for

Fig 57   The saw of the sawfish is a common trophy to be found in antique shops (the origin of the illustration). The teeth are embedded along each side of the long snout-like projection but far-removed from the mouth. Sawfish attain a length of upwards of 20ft of which the saw may be 6ft

holding it too, because all the backwardly directed teeth act as barbs and prevent the prey from slipping forward.

The teeth of the shark are of interest from the point of view of comparative anatomy. In the skin of sharks and dogfish there are embedded innumerable, sharp, backwardly pointed scales, called the placoid scales and there is a distinct correlation between these and the shark's teeth. It is most probable that the latter are indeed modified scales.

SEA-HORSES

The pipe fish are slow defenceless creatures which rely on their similarity to seaweeds to foil the predators. In addition, however, the body obtains some protection from a series of bony rings and plates with which it is encircled. The sea-horses are well known examples. The head is inclined at right-angles to the body and possesses a pipe-like snout. The tail is long and prehensile and is able to coil around the stems of seaweeds and other objects. The outer skeleton or rings and plates mentioned above allow the sea-horse body to dry intact and, indeed, extraordinary numbers of sea-horses are caught and dried for making up into brooches or for embedding in plastic for the tourist trade. Pipe fish constitute the family *Syngnathidae*.

Chapter 11

Reptiles of the Sea

The reptiles are most easily distinguished by their possession of horny scales usually covering the body completely. In some reptiles however, where the covering is not complete, the non-scaly areas are horny or at least very hard. These horny areas may contain bony plates as in the tortoises, turtles and crocodiles. The scaly or horny outer skin gives good protection, not only against injury from predators and accident, but also functions as a mechanism preventing desiccation. Those who have seen reptiles basking in the open in the heat of the tropics must be aware of this. Reptiles reached their zenith in the Mesozoic period, both in size and numbers. They were then the dominant animal class, but from that time they declined whilst birds and mammals increased in numbers. Whilst the reptiles showed an advance over the *Amphibia,* mainly due to an advance in the elaboration of the internal organs, the birds to a smaller extent and the mammals to a much larger extent, showed many advances over the structure of the reptiles. The living types of reptiles are relatively few compared with the numbers in the past. There are four main groups, not very closely related to each other. They are: *Chelonia,* tortoises and turtles; *Squamata,* lizards and snakes; *Crocodilia,* crocodiles and their relatives, and lastly the unique Tuatara of New Zealand.

Reptiles are cold-blooded and reach their highest numbers, both in species and actual abundance, in the tropics.

TURTLES

Amongst the reptiles, the turtles are those which we associate with the marine environment although, in fact, a few other reptiles are to be found scattered rather sparsely around the world's shores. The turtles are members of the reptile group *Chelonia* including also the tortoises of the land and freshwater. All *Chelonia* are characterised by the bony and horny exoskeleton which is known as the carapace on top, and the plastron beneath. Each is seen to be made up of a number of scale-like elements. Whereas in the land tortoises and freshwater tortoises, each limb is furnished with five claws, in the turtles the limbs are modified as paddles. The latter, together with the streamlined although scale-armoured body, makes the turtle a most efficient animal for swimming and finding its food in the seas and oceans of the world. But like all animals that have evolved from those that have already colonised the land, the turtles must return to the land to breed and, at this stage, it is at its most vulnerable period for predation at the hands of man.

He would indeed be a fortunate beachcomber who found the carapace of a turtle on a beach. For very many years however, these, as well as the whole dried animal, have been articles of decoration brought back by sailors from their voyages and thence finding their way into antique shops. The hawksbill turtle from which tortoiseshell was obtained at one time commercially, were often exhibited in opticians' shops as spectacle frames were made from this material. Turtles are very tenacious of life. They linger for weeks and often for months turned upside down on the deck of a ship. These gave the crew, or more often, the officers, fresh meat or if the ship was on the homeward run, they were sold in London and other city ports for making into turtle soup. Sometimes, the heads of particularly large turtles were mounted onto wooden shields in the manner of African game trophies.

The four principal species of turtles are the green turtle, *Chelone midas*, which is exclusively a vegetable feeder subsisting on various species of seaweeds and eel-grass, *Zostera*. The hawksbill, *Chelone imbricata*, the leathery turtle, *Dermochelys coriacea* and the logger-head, *Caretta caretta*, are all exclusively carnivorous and subsist on practically anything in the way of animal matter that they can get in the sea from medusae and salps to fish. All members of *Chelonia* however, are highly susceptible to temperature. Land tortoises hibernate in temperate climates, whilst the turtles are found only in the warm seas although they do wander into cooler water on occasion.

A return to land is made for breeding when the female turtles make their ungainly way up sandy shores to lay their golf-ball-sized eggs. A hole in the sand is scooped out for them and they are covered with sand when laid. The young turtles make their own way out of the sand on hatching, and flip their way back to the sea. Turtles and their eggs are edible, indeed they are considered delicacies to the extent that they have virtually disappeared from areas where once they were abundant. A number of breeding shores are however, now protected in order to help them regain former numbers.

CROCODILES

Most crocodiles are to be found in or around fresh water, and I have already described in my book *African Notebook* the finding of the skeletons of several crocodiles on the shores of a remote island in the Sese group in Lake Victoria. One crocodile species however, can be considered marine. At least it is to be found in salt water in estuaries and protected bays on the north coast of Australia. It is a species which grows to a very large size and when visiting Darwin in 1970, I saw the massive skull of one of these in the chemist's window.

Finally we should mention two other groups of reptiles found in the sea, although only of local distribution. Firstly, the sea-snakes, snakes which spend almost all their life in the sea – only coming ashore to breed. They are to be found in a few rather scattered tropical areas usually close to the shore. The water-cobra of East Africa spends most of its time in the fresh water Lake Tanganyika, and is sometimes found curled up under rocks on the shore.

MARINE IGUANA

The other main reptile not previously mentioned is the marine iguana of the Galapagos Islands in the Pacific. Although found nowhere else in the world, it is very common along the shores of the archipelago where hundreds lie draped over the rocks at the sea's edge. From time to time it enters the sea and swims out to feed on a species of seaweed. The water in the Humboldt current is relatively cool, so that after a period underwater it returns to the scorching hot rocks to warm up. There are a number of skeletons of these creatures around, but the Galapagos is an area heavily (and rightly) conserved and one may not pick up any animal alive or dead. The beachcombing in the Galapagos can only be in the mind or the memory and if you wish to collect then it must be only with the camera or pencil.

TUATARA

The Tuatara, which is lizard-like but anatomically only distantly related, is found today only on about a dozen small islands near the New Zealand mainland. They were formerly distributed more widely in New Zealand, but feral cats, rats and other predators caused them to become extinct by the middle of the nineteenth century. In their present island reserves they are rigorously protected. Only a few specimens have been exported during the last 40 years.

Chapter 12

Birds

The relationship of birds to reptiles can be seen by the presence of horny scales on the feet and legs, as well as a horny sheath on the beak of the birds. But, although showing such features of their reptilean ancestry, birds are the most highly specialised of the higher animals. The covering of non-conducting feathers, the possession of wings modified from the fore-limbs, massive muscles attached to a specially adapted sternum and shoulder-girdle, devices for lightening the weight of bones and internal organs, and the placing weight on the hind-limbs, are examples of this specialisation. Yet birds as a class are remarkably uniform as far as the essential features of their construction are concerned, in spite of the fact that they have become adapted to take advantage of greatly differing conditions.

BIRD ANATOMY

Birds, because of their mastery of flight, are common inhabitants of the oceans, or rather the air above them, and their shores. Many bird species exhibit extreme adaptations fitting them for life at sea, either for spending long periods in flight or for long periods spent swimming or diving. Some of the latter have entirely lost the power of flight such as the penguins, but their swimming capabilities are equal to those of fish. All birds however, must come to land to breed, and many oceanic birds are ill-adapted for this abrupt environmental change. The young fledged birds after spending many weeks and sometimes months at the bottom of a burrow or on a desolate island, must take to the sea or the air. For this reason there is often a high mortality amongst the young birds, and if the weather is harsh, their bodies are washed up onto the tide line within a few days of their launching into the air.

Fig 58   The skull of an albatross from Rottnest island off Western Australia.
Length: $7\frac{1}{4}$in

Exceptional mortality occurs for a number of other reasons. There must be few beachcombers who have not seen numbers of sea-birds killed through oil-pollution. Indeed, on occasion, this has reached extremely high proportions and those species that spend much time swimming on the sea's surface have been eliminated from the oiled areas. Often the skeletal parts of sea-birds remain on the beaches and when washed by the sea, abraded by the wind-blown sand and bleached by the sun, regain a beauty appreciated by the naturalist.

So that the beachcomber can also appreciate something of the story of adaptation which the bones of birds show, we must give a simple description of the skeleton of a bird. In common with all other backboned animals, almost without exception, the skeleton is divided into three distinct parts. Firstly the axial skeleton which consists of the skull and vertebral column or backbone. This latter is made up of a number of separate units which, to a greater or lesser degree articulate with each other. In birds it is the neck region which exhibits the greater flexibility, often to quite an astounding degree. The swan is an example and the long neck enables it to feed on the lake bottom when it 'up-ends'. Two particular units of the vertebral column, or vertebrae, are worthy of mention. Firstly the atlas or first vertebrae which supports the head and the second, known as the axis, which enables the head to rotate. Those vertebrae in the neck region are known as cervical, those of the back, dorsal, those of the hip or loins,

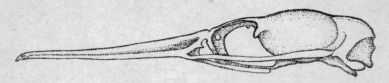

Fig 59   Skull of a shearwater, Dunmanus Bay, Ireland. Length of specimen: 4⅝in

pelvic or saural and those constituting the tail are called caudal vertebrae. In all but the well known fossil bird *Archeopteryx* however, all the caudal vertebrae are fused together. In many birds a number of the dorsal vertebrae are fused together also. The triangular mass of caudal vertebrae is called the pygostyle and carries the tail feathers. The remaining parts of the skeleton consist of the two girdles with their appendages and together they are known as the appendicular skeleton.

A feather is one of the most remarkable, and at the same time, one of the most beautiful things that nature has created. Feathers are to be found only as an external covering to the body and limbs of birds. They are to be found on no other animal groups. Feathers perform a number of highly important functions for birds. They streamline the bird, making the bird's body more aerodynamically effective. They extend the fore-limbs into 'wings' thereby converting them into efficient aerofoils. By trapping a layer of air, feathers insulate the bird's body in extremes of temperature and they waterproof the body so efficiently that a large number of bird species are able to live and obtain their food from a watery world. A very wide range of form and colour is to be found amongst the feathers of birds. In many species there is such a pattern of background colours that the birds are able to conceal themselves most effectively. There are a number of other functions too in which feathers are involved, courtship displays and egg incubation perhaps being the most important.

Feathers are epidermal structures formed from outgrowths of the skin and they are replaced at regular intervals. At the end of a season of flight many feathers become damaged so that replace-

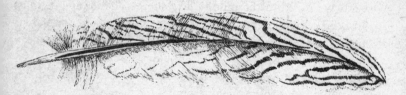

Fig 60   Feather of a silver pheasant 'beachcombed' from a forest where a fox
had probably devoured its owner

ment is usually necessary. Feathers are not produced evenly over the body except in the penguins, but arise from definite feather tracts, leaving quite large areas of the skin bare. But the direction of insertion into the skin and their length, ensures that the whole body is adequately covered.

Moulting of the feathers usually takes place after the season's brood has been reared and the parent birds can rest. Not all the feathers are moulted at the same time, of course, or the birds would be at the mercy both of predators and the elements. But from the middle to late summer, feathers are usually a feature of an English beach, and at corresponding times at other parts of the world. Additionally, birds killed by accident or by predators have their feathers scattered along the shore when the corpse is picked over by the carrion-eaters.

A collection of feathers is a harmless occupation, but one of greatest interest when sufficient expertise is garnered to make it possible to identify the bird and the particular type of feather. The shore is a wonderful place for picking up feathers. One of the most exciting shores for feathers that I have visited was at Lake Manyara in Tanzania. It is a large lake; the opposite shore was well out of sight but the near shallows was a shimmering white and pink of flamingos and pelicans. A large herd of buffalo snorted and splashed amongst some reeds at one end of the shore and at the other a herd of wildebeest cantered about in their characteristic hunchbacked fashion. In between was a large flat lawn-like area down which we drove the Land-Rover going as close as we dared to the muddy lake shore. The flamingos must have been moulting because the shore was covered with their feathers. Each looked as though its long pointed end had been dipped in some carmine coloured liquid. Most beautiful.

When a feather is picked up from the shore where it has lodged, perhaps in a bunch of seaweed drying on the high-tide mark, it is not sufficient to stuff it in a pocket. Although a feather is immensely strong for its weight and is able to perform an almost miraculous job in the air, it is nevertheless a most delicate object and if it becomes rubbed or is harshly treated it crumples and loses its beauty. Feathers should be placed in paper or plastic envelopes and carried in such a way that they cannot bend. On arrival home they should be stuck onto card and the date, place of collection, and name of collector, should be written on the card. If the name of the bird is known, then that should be included also. Such cards are best stored in an album made up of clear plastic 'pockets'.

PRESERVING FEATHERS

The insects that normally feed on feathers in old bird's nests can be a hazard to the collector. These include a number of species of moths, such as the clothes moths and house moths, and the carpet and furniture beetles. The larval or premature stage of these insects chew up feathers and when they are present can destroy a collection of feathers in a very short space of time. This can be prevented, and the specimens preserved, by spraying with an insecticide formulated for this purpose. Rentokil mothproofer aerosol contains lindane, and is ideal for the purpose. Its preserving effect lasts about a year.

OILED BIRDS

It is not to be assumed that everything found upon the beach is necessarily beautiful and exciting. Often there is sadness as well.

There can be few more pitiful sights than an oiled bird, a bird that has swum into an oil patch or 'slick', and whose feathers have become grossly contaminated. Extremely few birds survive this even if they happen to be picked up by kindly disposed people. It is heartening to learn, however, that more success is attending the efforts of those who have been studying the problems of oiled birds, and there are now a number of experts in de-oiling. One of the problems has been that the solvents used for dissolving contaminating oil also dissolves the natural water-repellent oils which allow a seabird to float and dive without becoming wet.

It is a most disagreeable sight to see a number of dead, oiled birds on a shoreline, and the beachcomber can help by reporting such birds to the local office of the RSPCA.

Mammals of the Sea

The *Mammalia* is the most highly developed class of animals. Mammals are characterised in all cases by the possession of lungs for breathing even in those where the usual habitat is aquatic. The temperature of the blood of mammals is high and constant, resembling that of birds but differing from reptiles, amphibia and fish. However, perhaps the most easily observed distinguishing feature of mammals is the presence of hair which replaces the scales and feathers of reptiles and birds. The young of mammals are born in the form of the adult with the exception of the monotremes of Australia (spiny anteater and duck-billed platypus) which lay eggs. When the young of mammals are born they are nourished by suckling at mammary or milk-glands. In the case of the marsupials of Australia, the young are born at a very early stage of development and make their way to mammary glands situated in a pouch at the base of the mother's abdomen.

Returning to the subject of the characteristic hair of mammals, the amount of hair present varies considerably. In most mammals the hair clothes the body almost completely as a dense fur, but on the other hand it may occur when the animal is young but thereafter lost, leaving only a few, such as the hairs in the elephant's tail.

There are three major groups of mammals associated with marine life; the whales and dolphins or *Cetacea*, the dugongs and manatees or *Sirenia*, and the seals and sealions or *Pinnipedia* section of the *Carnivora*. In the whales and dolphins hair is absent except for a few bristles in the vicinity of the mouth, but the young are suckled. This group contains some of the largest of living mammals and are fish-like in appearance except for the horizontal position of the tail-flukes, whereas the tail is vertical in fish. The nostrils are paired in the whalebone whales, but in the toothed whales, porpoises and dolphins the nostrils unite to form a single crescent-shaped aperture. In the dugongs and manatees the body is somewhat less fish-like, although the hind-limbs are united to form a single horizontal fin. Hair is very sparse. The *Pinnipedia* on the other hand are generously supplied with hair. The upper canine teeth of the walruses are greatly enlarged and project downwards. They may sometimes be picked up in antique shops.

WHALES AND DOLPHINS

Spending the whole of their lives in the sea, the whales and dolphins are the mammals best suited for life in the sea. Stranding in shallow waters is dangerous, and even lethal, for some species such as the killer whale and sperm whale, as their great weight causes the chest cavity to deform and they suffocate. Normally whales avoid inshore waters. The blue whale, *Balaenoptera musculus*, is the largest living animal and reaches a length of 100ft. It was some years ago that I came across the skull of a whale on a beach. This was at Blakeney Point in Norfolk. Happily the sea had washed the bone quite clean but, unfortunately, I did not have my drawing equipment with me so that I could not record its impression upon me. It was far too large to carry away and far too remote to get any sort of transport near it. I tried its weight but I could not budge it. I don't know whether I would have had any legal right to it in any case.

WHALEBONE

The first thing we should state about whalebone is that it is not, in fact, bone. Whalebone is a horny substance produced by the epithelium lining the mouth. It is now more generally referred to as baleen and it is produced by a group of whales known as the right whales, whalebone whales, or *Mysteceti*.
Each piece of baleen is roughly triangular and blade-like in shape and may be as much as 13ft in length. Most often it is black in colour but may be quite pale or even whitish. The long edge of

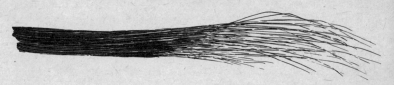

Fig 61   A piece of baleen or whalebone fringed at the end. Planktonic animals, mainly crustaceans, are caught on the horny fibres and then swallowed. Strips cut from the springy basal part of the baleen were used in the manufacture of ladies' corsets before the introduction of steel springs

each of the 300 or so blades is considerably frayed, forming a sieve through which the water is strained and the planktonic organisms retained as food. The whalebone whales subsist entirely on the small animal organisms, mostly crustacea, swimming near the surface of the sea, known as the plankton.

In the days of poor communications great mystery attended the origin of whalebone. It was thought that it was the eyelashes of the whale, or that it was the fin. Whalebone was of great value in days gone by. In 1897 it was sold for £2,000 per ton and a medium-sized whale would contain several tons of the material. When a right whale was washed up on shore the beachcomber who found it was able to make a fortune (if he could keep it to himself)!

THE TOOTHED WHALES

This group, known as the *Odontoceti*, do not have whalebone, but the jaws are furnished with teeth. It includes the dolphins and porpoises which are from 4ft to less than 20ft in length, and also the huge sperm whale, *Physeter catodon*, which may be up to 60ft in length.

The bottlenosed dolphin, *Tursiops truncatus*, is familiar to many on account of their being kept in large aquaria. It reaches a length of 14ft. Gus Angermeyer, of Santa Cruz, who possessed the largest collection of beachcombed material in his cave on Santa

Cruz Island in the Galapagos that I have ever seen, gave me a skull of the Pacific species, *T. gilli*. It is probably very old as it has a strange chalky texture. The blow-holes at the top of the head, and the long, sloping beak of the upper jaw, are characteristic of the dolphins.

The common dolphin, *Delphinus delphis*, is usually seen in large schools of sixty or more. It grows to a length of about 8ft and is extremely agile. When travelling fast, they regularly leap completely out of the water several feet into the air. They are to be found in temperate seas in many parts of the world. My grandson found a skull of this species in Dunmanus Bay in south-west Ireland. The beaches in this beautiful area are very well worth exploring by the beachcomber.

SPERM WHALE TEETH

Various parts of whales, at least some species, have become collectable items and should be the quarry of the beachcomber, although the chances of finding them on the beaches today are pretty slender. The teeth of the sperm whale are to be found in many sorts of junk and antique shops, but those that have been decorated or carved by the old Nantucket whalers are usually very expensive and are to be found only at the top end of the antique trade. But sometimes one can acquire a few teeth quite cheaply if you know what you are looking for and you are capable of discerning them from amongst a mass of other stuff. The sperm teeth vary enormously in size as they progress along the jaw and the old ones, when cut longitudinally, reveal a most beautiful marbled pattern.

THE TUSK OF THE NARWAAL

The narwaal is a smallish whale, at least when we consider the general size of whales. It usually grows to a length of about 15ft, but the remarkable feature of this species is that a long spirally curled tusk is carried by the male. It consists of the specially

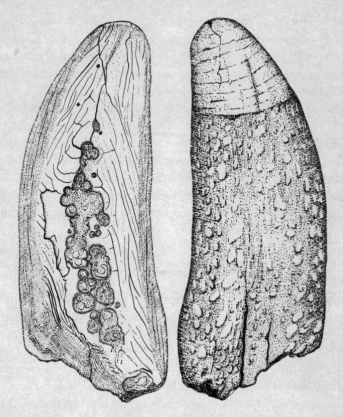

Fig 62   An old tooth of the sperm whale. *Left*, sectioned; *right*, view of outer surface. Tooth is 8½in in length

modified upper incisor tooth and is thus a secondary sexual character. As to its function, however, many theories have been advanced, but none so far appear to have been generally accepted. Male narwaals have been seen 'fencing' but whether it is an offensive or defensive weapon seems open to doubt. In size they are several feet in length and consist of very dense ivory.

It is very likely that the tusks of the narwaal gave rise to the myth of the unicorn. The narwaal certainly only bears one 'horn', but its body cannot be considered horse-like by any stretch of the imagination. But it is no myth that the Asiatic peoples believed in the narwaal's tusk as possessing strong aphrodisiac properties. The ivory was ground up into a powder and swallowed by elderly gentlemen. Another early belief was that a cup made of the ivory from the narwaal tusk was capable of distinguishing poison from wine – quite a useful piece of equipment in those far-off days! Today, one would be very fortunate to find a narwaal cast up on a beach, only two or three are known from the British coasts. The tusk, however, is an object of curiosity and, in spite of its present-day rarity, of commerce also.

In the past, the narwaal tusk was used by the Eskimo hunter as a spear, lance or harpoon. Those of the latter can be distinguished by the narrow groove which has been cut a little distance from the sharp end in order to secure a barb and a thong for recovery. With this weapon the seal could be hunted. The tusk has also been used as the regalia of office. One is used as the central shaft for the mace of the Canadian parliament.

In the early 1950s tusks of the narwaal were common objects in the antique shops and were inexpensive. I am ashamed to say that I paid only seven shillings and sixpence for my own tusk which is 54in long. It has been used as an Eskimo harpoon and, no doubt, has seen some years of freezing use. A few years ago, however, they rather suddenly became collectors' items and were advertised for in *The Times*. I was offered £20 for mine but I thought I would one day like to draw and write about narwaal tusks and I held on to it. I believe a number were bought together for the décor of a restaurant in some Scandinavian country. The upshot of this has been that their value has climbed higher and higher. The last one I saw was in a high class antique shop in Belgravia – the asking price was £75! All I can say is keep your weather eye open for one that has somehow been overlooked.

AMBERGRIS

This wax-like substance of ashy, marbled colour, was formerly one of the valuable beachcombing finds. It is a secretion of the sperm whale and it is to be found in its intestines. Often the horny beaks of cuttlefish are embedded in it.

It is interesting to note that the word amber was originally given to this substance, then, when the name was given also to the resin, the secretion was differentiated as *ambergris*. In the past there has been a great deal of confusion between ambergris and spermaceti. This latter is a fatty substance which when it has been purified appears as a soft white scaly mass. It is found in the head, and to a much lesser extent, in other parts of the sperm whale, and again to a lesser extent in other whales and dolphins. It is used for pharmaceutical preparations, and also in candle manufacture. Ambergris, on the other hand is, or was, used in perfumery.

SEALS, SEALIONS AND WALRUSES

These marine mammals constitute the *Pinnipedia*, which are sometimes considered to be part of the order *Carnivora* and sometimes to be quite distinct from it. There are three families, as follows:

1 *Otariidae*, with small well-developed ears, a long clearly defined neck which allows visibility in any direction, and with hind-limbs which can be brought forward and which can serve as hind-feet. The sealions and fur seals belong to this group.

2 *Odobenidae*, in which the walrus, *Odobenus rosmarus*, is the only species, and which is well known for its possession (in both sexes) of large, downward projecting tusks which are the highly modified upper canine teeth. The muzzle is flat and evenly covered with very strong but highly sensitive bristles. The tusks of the walrus, which may in the male reach a length of 3ft, have been items for the antique collector for many years, especially interesting for those collecting items of navigation and exploration. Although at one time present in large numbers around the whole length of the Arctic shoreline, there has been a great reduction in this species, which today is estimated to be between 50,000 and 100,000.

3 *Phocidae*, in which an external ear is absent and the hind-limbs point backwards, unable to be brought forward thus being of little use for propulsion when on land. Members of this group are widely distributed throughout the seas and oceans of the world, and are even present in some lakes, such as Baikal in Russia and in landlocked seas, such as the Caspian.

Some species, formerly abundant, are now rare, but others occur in such numbers that culling operations are thought desirable on account of their interference with inshore fishing.

Two seal species occur in British waters. These are the common or harbour seal, *Phoca vitulina*, and the grey or Atlantic seal, *Halichoerus grypus*. The former is distributed along the coastlines of the north Atlantic and north Pacific, but the latter in the north Atlantic only. Around the shores of the North American continent, 13 species of seals and sealions occur, as well as the walrus. Many species of *Pinnipedia* congregate at breeding time in large numbers, usually on unfrequented beaches difficult of access except from the sea. Many animals die or are killed at this time, and their remains become scattered along the shore. If the beachcomber is stench-tolerant, he might find skulls and other bony elements for his collection.

Other than marine mammals such as whales, porpoises and seals, the skeletal parts of many terrestrial mammals are often found along the shoreline. The bodies of land mammals often get washed down rivers to the sea during flooding and at other times, and after a time get deposited on a beach. The otter is an aquatic mammal which spends some of the time in coastal regions and at other times frequents rivers and streams. In recent years a serious decline in their numbers has been reported and as a consequence a survey of the otter population has been made. Strangely, although I have never found an otter's skull, that of a badger has been found on the shore by my grandson then aged three. Amongst many stones on the beach, he ran and fetched the whitest. This was on a beach in Dunmanus Bay in south-west Ireland and a subsequent search revealed two pelvic girdles of badgers and a number of other bones, but I never found the second skull.

THE QUOKKA

One of the main reasons why a visit to the island of Rottnest was eagerly anticipated apart from the pleasures of beachcombing, was the opportunity of seeing the quokka or short-tailed wallaby,

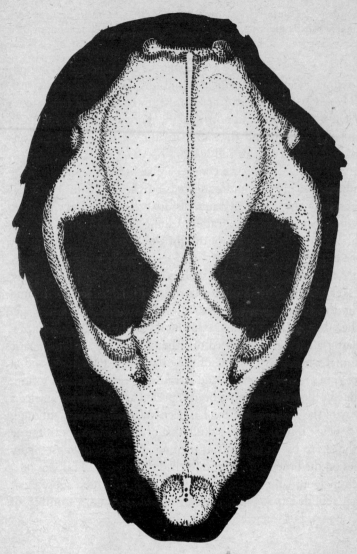

Fig 63   Badger skull from the shore at Reenmore. South-west Ireland. 5in

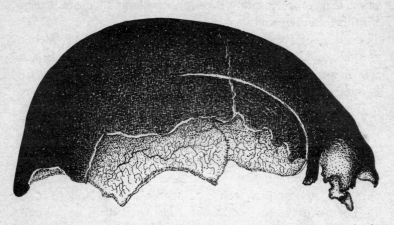

Fig 64   Cranium of a human skull from the Nyenga desert, Kenya. Only the tip of the nasal region projected from the sand

a marsupial of very restricted distribution. Indeed it is confined to the islands of Rottnest and Bald and a few isolated pockets on the Western Australian mainland. When we arrived on Rottnest we asked how we could see the quokkas. 'Just make a noise like a piece of bread' we were informed and, when we arrived at the settlement, we saw our first quokkas and were disgusted to find them feeding on rubbish around the dustbins. Although nocturnal animals, they were sorting out the crusts and fruit waste and taking them under the huts (which were built about a couple of feet above the ground) to consume them. The quokka is a stockily built, grey-brown rat-like animal with rounded ears. It has a very short tapering tail, very small fore-legs and large hind-legs. It jumps or hops along on the latter in typical kangaroo style, and sits about in hunched-up style. We saw a number of them around the island usually sheltering from the sun in the thick shrub layer of sedges, sand-dune plants and tea-trees. All along the shore we saw their tracks where they had been beachcombing for eatable refuse and they must have been present in thousands. This animal is considered a pest by Rottnesters as they are so numerous on the island that no treeplanting is possible without adequate fencing. Visitors feed them and they show little fear of man.

The island of Rottnest lies 12 miles off the coast of Western Australia and is some 7 miles in length and 3 in breadth. Its total area is something less than 5,000 acres. The history of its first sightings, landings and wrecks makes fascinating but tragic reading. The *Golden Dragon* sailing from Texel to Batavia went off course to the south and six months after sailing was wrecked on 28 April 1656 on Rottnest. In a rescue attempt in 1658 fourteen men were marooned due to the loss of boats during a storm. Four of these men survived and indeed arrived in Batavia only four months after their commander Samuel Volkersen. He did not name the island. This was left to Willem de Vlaming who landed on the island in 1696. After a voyage of several months Vlaming wrote of Rottnest 'Here it seems that nature has spared nothing to render this isle delightful above all others that I have ever seen.' However, he said that there were no animals except a 'kind of rat as big as a common cat whose dung is found in abundance all over the island'.

Chapter 14

The Beachcomber
as an Illustrator

A book on beachcombing, where so many natural objects of great beauty are described and illustrated, is probably a good place in which to write down the method of drawing which the author employs.

Making one's own pictures of finds on the beach is an interesting and satisfying way of using one's leisure. Not only that, but when one comes to draw even such a simple object as a shell, one becomes aware of intricate detail perhaps associated with growth or attachment. This would perhaps have gone unnoticed had not extra concentrated observation been given to the object so that a drawing could be made.

In drawing, everyone creates their own style. If one thousand artists sat down to draw one single object, the result would be one thousand different drawings, each of which could be scientifically accurate. Each artist, however, would render his own impression of the texture and form and even the outline in his own way. A drawing, in a sense, can only be a cartoon. In drawing a leaf, for example, it would be impossible to draw in every hair or every vein even though we had good enough eyes to see them. So that we draw in such a way that denotes or suggests a hairy appearance or a fine reticulation of veins. Similarly, in drawing a mouse we would not, nor could we, draw every hair.

Drawing nature has been the author's own leisure-time pursuit over many years, and the particular technique of drawing which has been employed is simple to master. It is the author's earnest wish that the reader will try it out for himself or herself. A word of encouragement – no matter what degree of expertise in drawing is possessed by the reader, scraperboard drawing improves the

Fig 65   The *Radix murex* is a most attractive mollusc with its dove-grey shell and blunt black spines. The shell is up to 4in long.

Fig 66   The pen or fan shells are often very large but are also very fragile. The giant Mediterranean pen, *Pinna nobilis*, grows up to 14in in length but needs careful packing to get it home without breakage

Fig 67   The worm shells, *Vermicularia* species, are at first rather like the turret shells, but then the whorls have the appearance of being unwound, and resemble the cases of marine worms. Specimen is nearly 5in long

appearance of the final result. The exhilarating feeling of walking along shores is increased by the enjoyment of finding natural objects thrown onto the beach by the tide. It is increased still further when an object has been identified and something learned of its biology. But, when a drawing has been made of it and a few notes about the circumstances of its collection added, then an heirloom has been created.

SCRAPERBOARD DRAWING

As a very small boy I was interested in drawing. In those days we drew natural growing things such as horse chestnut buds, 'sticky buds', crocus flowers bursting from their corms, 'pussy' willows, or in the autumn we painted the crimson fiery leaves of virginia creeper. We tried with painstaking detail to make our painting or drawing look as near to the living thing as our limited techniques permitted. In the intervening years art took control, but in spite of this I went on drawing nature as it appeared to me. After many years of illustrating papers on caddis fly larvae, and undesirable insect species in buildings in the conventional manner of mapping pen, indian ink and bristol-board, with all its limitations (and I was never able to aspire to the heights of this technique as reached by Dr Hugh Cott), the scraperboard material for line illustrating was introduced to me. This so fitted what I wanted to do in the way of illustrating, not only scientific papers but newspaper articles and books, that I have used it ever since and, furthermore,

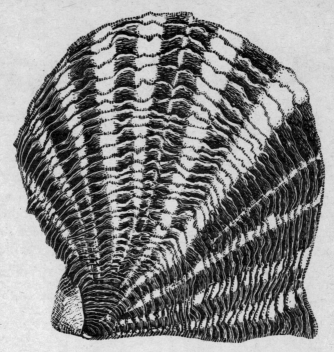

Fig 68   The black-lipped oyster, *Pinctada margaritifera*, is one of the six species able to produce precious pearls. It grows up to 6in across and is to be found growing in many areas of south-east Asia where the sea bottom is rocky

I have adapted it to my own personal inclinations in drawing. Anyone else, of course, can do the same because it is a very plastic medium in the sense that it allows of a very wide interpretation of what one wants to convey, as an illustration, to the printed page.

I suppose one of the great influences over me, in taking up scraperboard, was the remarkable number of illustrations, using this technique, which C. F. Tunnicliffe produced. The great masses of black on the page affected me very much and I would sit for a long time looking at the page on which sat the drawing! I came to the conclusion that a square line around the drawing improved it. Indeed, Tunnicliffe did without 'squaring them up' and over-

Fig 69   The lion's paw scallop, *Lyropecten podosus*, from the Caribbean region
grows up to 5in in length and is brown to reddish-brown in colour

leaf, only the bottom half of the drawing is squared.

My first two completed scraperboard drawings were of a stag beetle and a badger, both of which I used as Christmas cards, and are published in *Forest Refreshed*. I was disappointed with the square box in which they both appeared to sit, so I made an irregular outline around them in each case.

Briefly, scraperboard itself is a very heavily chalked surface on a thin paper backing. In fact, it could be described as a thin layer of chalk on a very thin layer of paper. It is very fragile, so much so that one must not bend or drop the sheet of scraperboard otherwise it will crack or break. One excellent way of protecting it is

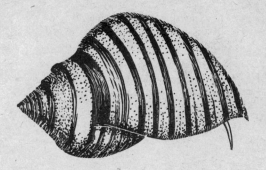

Fig 70 *Delphinula* snails are often ornamented with long curved spines and variously shaped excrescences. This species, *Delphinula angeria*, is from the Philippines and is purple in colour

to keep it always, and transport it always, in a plastic carrying case with clear plastic pockets.

This is, in fact, not such a burden as it sounds, as such cases are readily available and can be used for sending scraperboard drawings through the post without any further protection, except to put it into a large envelope or a simple brown paper covering. Many hundreds of scraperboard drawings have been sent through the post in such plastic carrying cases, to editors and publishers, over something like twenty years without any mishap taking place. Unfortunately, in spite of notices placed in the cases, that all the enclosed drawings must be returned in the special case provided, there is an exceptionally heavy wastage in this respect. The artist, however, must be philosophical about this and consider that the plastic case has done its job by delivering the drawings to the printer in first class condition.

Now that we have described what the scraperboard consists of and how it should be handled, how does one go about using it? In the first place the scraperboard can be purchased either in black or white. If one is going to use a predominantly black background then the former is purchased. Personally, I do not suppose that in a thousand drawings has a black background been used more than ten times, but strangely this is what jumps into a number of

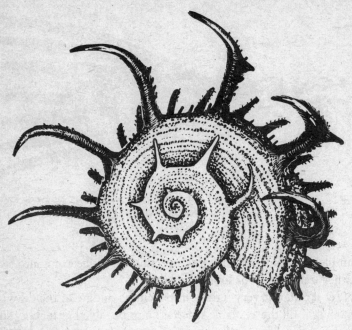

Fig 71 *Opeastoma pseudodon*, a carnivorous species from West Mexico which
opens bivalve molluscs with its long curved tooth

people's minds if you tell them that you employ the scraperboard technique. In fact, the black background, or silhouette, as I prefer to call it, is brushed on just where it is required, using a small watercolour brush (such as a Windsor and Newton Sable No 6) and indian ink. Then let it dry.

We should perhaps say something about the size of the drawing. The author has always found it convenient to have the scraperboard cut to a standard size, for several reasons. For one thing, if the drawing is always done to a certain size, one learns from experience how the drawing will reduce for publication. Generally, drawings of line illustration are reduced to half or one-third for the printed illustration. The standard size of drawing paper preferred by the author was 8in x 10in, quarto size, in fact; although it must be confessed that in the case of comparatively

Fig 72   An eel spear fashioned out of one piece of iron for screwing into a
wooden shaft

simple drawings, shells for instance, this size has been cut into two, either transversely or longitudinally.

Now sketch out very lightly in pencil the outline of the drawing making it fill the available space as far as possible but making sure that tails, bristles, or other space consumers, are accommodated on the page. On a few occasions it has been my experience to complete a drawing on two separate pieces of scraperboard, then fasten them together with tape. They have caused much embarrassment to all concerned. On one occasion the two halves were thought to be two separate illustrations! Then the drawing should be divided up according to the type of background, and where this is to be black it should be inked in as described earlier. It is often a good plan to outline the drawing in indian ink using a mapping pen. It is then quicker and more accurate to apply the ink within the outline by brush. The next stage is for the ink to dry which may take up to about an hour, but a few minutes in front of an electric fire, even in the dead of winter usually suffices. The next stage is to scrape off the unwanted black ink. This is very easily carried out and one usually gathers in mounted needles in holders, razor blades, old knives and sundry sharpened hardware that one knows from experience are just right for the job (although of course art shops do sell special sets of cutting tools as well). As one cuts, scrapes, pricks, prods or pecks, so a gentle blow disperses the chalk dust which has been removed. It will be found at the outset that there is much greater control over such implements than over a mapping pen carrying wet indian ink, so that the work is carried out to a much greater degree of fineness or accuracy. It is far, far easier to peck out a pattern of fine white spots on a black background on scraperboard than it is to put black dots on bristol-board.

One important thing about black and white drawing, you can make it look more like the object than it really is!

So, armed with sketching materials and the knowledge gleaned from this book, you are now ready to realise the endless possibilities of a seemingly 'empty' beach.

Further Reading

Abbot, R. T. *Sea Shells of the World* (1962)

Austin, O. L. *Birds of the World* (1961)

Burt, W. H. and Grossenheider, R. P. *A Field Guide to the Mammals* (Boston, 1952)

Bustard, R. *Sea Turtles* (1972)

Guppy, H. B. *Plants, Seeds and Currents in the West Indies and Azores* (1917)

King J. E. *Seals of the World* (1964)

Le Danois, E. *Marine Life of Coastal Waters* (1957)

McMillan, N. F. *British Shells* (1968)

Norman, J. R. *A History of Fishes* (2nd ed P. H. Greenwood, 1963)

Rendell, J. *Flower Arrangement with a Marine Theme* (Newton Abbot, 1967)

Schmidt, K. P. and Inger, R. F. *Living Reptiles of the World* (1957)

Stephen, D., ed. *Dolphins, Seals and Other Sea Mammals* (Glasgow, 1973)

Strasburger. *Text-book of Botany*; many English editions since 1898

Tweedie, M. (Introduction) *Sea Shells* (1971)

Acknowledgements

Much of the material in this book was first published in a series of articles in the *Worcester Evening News*, and I wish to thank the editor, Mr Leon Hickman for permission to republish it. Thanks must also be given to Mrs Hilda Maxwell for the main bulk of typing and also to Mrs Pamela Willis for secretarial assistance.

Index

INDEX

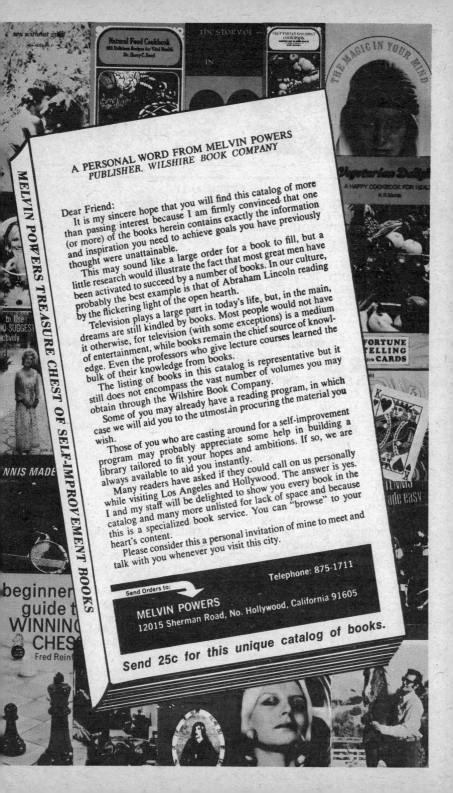

A PERSONAL WORD FROM MELVIN POWERS
PUBLISHER, WILSHIRE BOOK COMPANY

Dear Friend:

It is my sincere hope that you will find this catalog of more than passing interest because I am firmly convinced that one (or more) of the books herein contains exactly the information and inspiration you need to achieve goals you have previously thought were unattainable.

This may sound like a large order for a book to fill, but a little research would illustrate the fact that most great men have been activated to succeed by a number of books. In our culture, probably the best example is that of Abraham Lincoln reading by the flickering light of the open hearth.

Television plays a large part in today's life, but, in the main, dreams are still kindled by books. Most people would not have it otherwise, for television (with some exceptions) is a medium of entertainment, while books remain the chief source of knowledge. Even the professors who give lecture courses learned the bulk of their knowledge from books.

The listing of books in this catalog is representative but it still does not encompass the vast number of volumes you may obtain through the Wilshire Book Company.

Some of you may already have a reading program, in which case we will aid you to the utmost in procuring the material you wish.

Those of you who are casting around for a self-improvement program may probably appreciate some help in building a library tailored to fit your hopes and ambitions. If so, we are always available to aid you instantly.

Many readers have asked if they could call on us personally while visiting Los Angeles and Hollywood. The answer is yes. I and my staff will be delighted to show you every book in the catalog and many more unlisted for lack of space and because this is a specialized book service. You can "browse" to your heart's content.

Please consider this a personal invitation of mine to meet and talk with you whenever you visit this city.

Telephone: 875-1711

Send Orders to:

MELVIN POWERS
12015 Sherman Road, No. Hollywood, California 91605

Send 25c for this unique catalog of books.

MELVIN POWERS TREASURE CHEST OF SELF-IMPROVEMENT BOOKS

Melvin Powers
SELF-IMPROVEMENT
LIBRARY

ASTROLOGY

_____ASTROLOGY: A FASCINATING HISTORY *P. Naylor*   2.00
_____ASTROLOGY: HOW TO CHART YOUR HOROSCOPE *Max Heindel*   2.00
_____ASTROLOGY: YOUR PERSONAL SUN-SIGN GUIDE *Beatrice Ryder*   2.0
_____ASTROLOGY FOR EVERYDAY LIVING *Janet Harris*   2.00
_____ASTROLOGY MADE EASY *Astarte*   2.00
_____ASTROLOGY MADE PRACTICAL *Alexandra Kayhle*   2.00
_____ASTROLOGY, ROMANCE, YOU AND THE STARS *Anthony Norvell*   3.00
_____MY WORLD OF ASTROLOGY *Sydney Omarr*   3.00
_____THOUGHT DIAL *Sydney Omarr*   2.00
_____ZODIAC REVEALED *Rupert Gleadow*   2.00

BRIDGE & POKER

_____ADVANCED POKER STRATEGY & WINNING PLAY *A. D. Livingston*   2.00
_____BRIDGE BIDDING MADE EASY *Edwin Kantar*   5.00
_____BRIDGE CONVENTIONS *Edwin Kantar*   4.00
_____COMPLETE DEFENSIVE BRIDGE PLAY *Edwin B. Kantar*   10.00
_____HOW TO IMPROVE YOUR BRIDGE *Alfred Sheinwold*   2.00
_____HOW TO WIN AT POKER *Terence Reese & Anthony T. Watkins*   2.00
_____SECRETS OF WINNING POKER *George S. Coffin*   3.00
_____TEST YOUR BRIDGE PLAY *Edwin B. Kantar*   3.00

BUSINESS STUDY & REFERENCE

_____CONVERSATION MADE EASY *Elliot Russell*   2.0
_____EXAM SECRET *Dennis B. Jackson*   2.0
_____FIX-IT BOOK *Arthur Symons*   2.0
_____HOW TO DEVELOP A BETTER SPEAKING VOICE *M. Hellier*   2.0
_____HOW TO MAKE A FORTUNE IN REAL ESTATE *Albert Winnikoff*   3.0
_____HOW TO MAKE MONEY IN REAL ESTATE *Stanley L. McMichael*   2.0
_____INCREASE YOUR LEARNING POWER *Geoffrey A. Dudley*   2.0
_____MAGIC OF NUMBERS *Robert Tocquet*   2.0
_____PRACTICAL GUIDE TO BETTER CONCENTRATION *Melvin Powers*   2.0
_____PRACTICAL GUIDE TO PUBLIC SPEAKING *Maurice Forley*   2.0
_____7 DAYS TO FASTER READING *William S. Schaill*   2.0
_____SONGWRITERS' RHYMING DICTIONARY *Jane Shaw Whitfield*   3.0
_____SPELLING MADE EASY *Lester D. Basch & Dr. Milton Finkelstein*   2.0
_____STUDENT'S GUIDE TO BETTER GRADES *J. A. Rickard*   2.0
_____TEST YOURSELF — Find Your Hidden Talent *Jack Shafer*   2.0
_____YOUR WILL & WHAT TO DO ABOUT IT *Attorney Samuel G. Kling*   2.0

CHESS & CHECKERS

_____BEGINNER'S GUIDE TO WINNING CHESS *Fred Reinfeld*   2.0
_____BETTER CHESS — How to Play *Fred Reinfeld*   2.0
_____CHECKERS MADE EASY *Tom Wiswell*   2.0
_____CHESS IN TEN EASY LESSONS *Larry Evans*   2.0
_____CHESS MADE EASY *Milton L. Hanauer*   2.0
_____CHESS MASTERY — A New Approach *Fred Reinfeld*   2.0
_____CHESS PROBLEMS FOR BEGINNERS *edited by Fred Reinfeld*   2.0
_____CHESS SECRETS REVEALED *Fred Reinfeld*   2.0

Melvin Powers
SELF-IMPROVEMENT
LIBRARY

CHESS STRATEGY — An Expert's Guide *Fred Reinfeld*	2.00
CHESS TACTICS FOR BEGINNERS *edited by Fred Reinfeld*	2.00
CHESS THEORY & PRACTICE *Morry & Mitchell*	2.00
HOW TO WIN AT CHECKERS *Fred Reinfeld*	2.00
1001 BRILLIANT WAYS TO CHECKMATE *Fred Reinfeld*	2.00
1001 WINNING CHESS SACRIFICES & COMBINATIONS *Fred Reinfeld*	3.00
SOVIET CHESS *Edited by R. G. Wade*	3.00

COOKERY & HERBS

CULPEPER'S HERBAL REMEDIES *Dr. Nicholas Culpeper*	2.00
FAST GOURMET COOKBOOK *Poppy Cannon*	2.50
HEALING POWER OF HERBS *May Bethel*	2.00
HERB HANDBOOK *Dawn MacLeod*	2.00
HERBS FOR COOKING AND HEALING *Dr. Donald Law*	2.00
HERBS FOR HEALTH How to Grow & Use Them *Louise Evans Doole*	2.00
HOME GARDEN COOKBOOK Delicious Natural Food Recipes *Ken Kraft*	3.00
MEDICAL HERBALIST *edited by Dr. J. R. Yemm*	3.00
NATURAL FOOD COOKBOOK *Dr. Harry C. Bond*	2.00
NATURE'S MEDICINES *Richard Lucas*	2.00
VEGETABLE GARDENING FOR BEGINNERS *Hugh Wiberg*	2.00
VEGETABLES FOR TODAY'S GARDENS *R. Milton Carleton*	2.00
VEGETARIAN COOKERY *Janet Walker*	2.00
VEGETARIAN COOKING MADE EASY & DELECTABLE *Veronica Vezza*	2.00
VEGETARIAN DELIGHTS — A Happy Cookbook for Health *K. R. Mehta*	2.00
VEGETARIAN GOURMET COOKBOOK *Joyce McKinnel*	2.00

HEALTH

DR. LINDNER'S SPECIAL WEIGHT CONTROL METHOD	1.00
GAYELORD HAUSER'S NEW GUIDE TO INTELLIGENT REDUCING	3.00
HELP YOURSELF TO BETTER SIGHT *Margaret Darst Corbett*	2.00
HOW TO IMPROVE YOUR VISION *Dr. Robert A. Kraskin*	2.00
HOW YOU CAN STOP SMOKING PERMANENTLY *Ernest Caldwell*	2.00
LSD — THE AGE OF MIND *Bernard Roseman*	2.00
MIND OVER PLATTER *Peter G. Lindner, M.D.*	2.00
NEW CARBOHYDRATE DIET COUNTER *Patti Lopez-Pereira*	1.00
PSYCHEDELIC ECSTASY *William Marshall & Gilbert W. Taylor*	2.00
YOU CAN LEARN TO RELAX *Dr. Samuel Gutwirth*	2.00
YOUR ALLERGY—What To Do About It *Allan Knight, M.D.*	2.00

HOBBIES

BLACKSTONE'S MODERN CARD TRICKS *Harry Blackstone*	2.00
BLACKSTONE'S SECRETS OF MAGIC *Harry Blackstone*	2.00
COIN COLLECTING FOR BEGINNERS *Burton Hobson & Fred Reinfeld*	2.00
400 FASCINATING MAGIC TRICKS YOU CAN DO *Howard Thurston*	3.00
GOULD'S GOLD & SILVER GUIDE TO COINS *Maurice Gould*	2.00
HOW I TURN JUNK INTO FUN AND PROFIT *Sari*	3.00
HOW TO WRITE A HIT SONG & SELL IT *Tommy Boyce*	7.00
JUGGLING MADE EASY *Rudolf Dittrich*	2.00
MAGIC MADE EASY *Byron Wels*	2.00

_____SEXUALLY ADEQUATE FEMALE Frank S. Caprio, M.D.   2.00
_____SEXUALLY ADEQUATE MALE Frank S. Caprio, M.D.   2.00
_____YOUR FIRST YEAR OF MARRIAGE Dr. Tom McGinnis   2.00

METAPHYSICS & OCCULT

_____BOOK OF TALISMANS, AMULETS & ZODIACAL GEMS William Pavitt   3.00
_____CONCENTRATION—A Guide to Mental Mastery Mouni Sadhu   3.00
_____DREAMS & OMENS REVEALED Fred Gettings   2.00
_____EXTRASENSORY PERCEPTION Simeon Edmunds   2.00
_____FORTUNE TELLING WITH CARDS P. Foli   2.00
_____HANDWRITING ANALYSIS MADE EASY John Marley   2.00
_____HANDWRITING TELLS Nadya Olyanova   3.00
_____HOW TO UNDERSTAND YOUR DREAMS Geoffrey A. Dudley   2.00
_____ILLUSTRATED YOGA William Zorn   2.00
_____IN DAYS OF GREAT PEACE Mouni Sadhu   2.00
_____KING SOLOMON'S TEMPLE IN THE MASONIC TRADITION Alex Horne 5.00
_____MAGICIAN — His training and work W. E. Butler   2.00
_____MEDITATION Mouni Sadhu   3.00
_____MODERN NUMEROLOGY Morris C. Goodman   2.00
_____NUMEROLOGY—ITS' FACTS AND SECRETS Ariel Yvon Taylor   2.00
_____PALMISTRY MADE EASY Fred Gettings   2.00
_____PALMISTRY MADE PRACTICAL Elizabeth Daniels Squire   3.00
_____PALMISTRY SECRETS REVEALED Henry Frith   2.00
_____PRACTICAL YOGA Ernest Wood   3.00
_____PROPHECY IN OUR TIME Martin Ebon   2.50
_____PSYCHOLOGY OF HANDWRITING Nadya Olyanova   2.00
_____SEEING INTO THE FUTURE Harvey Day   2.00
_____SUPERSTITION — Are you superstitious? Eric Maple   2.00
_____TAROT Mouni Sadhu   4.00
_____TAROT OF THE BOHEMIANS Papus   3.00
_____TEST YOUR ESP Martin Ebon   2.00
_____WAYS TO SELF-REALIZATION Mouni Sadhu   2.00
_____WITCHCRAFT, MAGIC & OCCULTISM—A Fascinating History W. B. Crow 3.00
_____WITCHCRAFT — THE SIXTH SENSE Justine Glass   2.00
_____WORLD OF PSYCHIC RESEARCH Hereward Carrington   2.00
_____YOU CAN ANALYZE HANDWRITING Robert Holder   2.00

SELF-HELP & INSPIRATIONAL

_____CYBERNETICS WITHIN US Y. Saparina   3.00
_____DAILY POWER FOR JOYFUL LIVING Dr. Donald Curtis   2.00
_____DOCTOR PSYCHO-CYBERNETICS Maxwell Maltz, M.D.   3.00
_____DYNAMIC THINKING Melvin Powers   1.00
_____GREATEST POWER IN THE UNIVERSE U. S. Andersen   4.00
_____GROW RICH WHILE YOU SLEEP Ben Sweetland   2.00
_____GROWTH THROUGH REASON Albert Ellis, Ph.D.   3.00
_____GUIDE TO DEVELOPING YOUR POTENTIAL Herbert A. Otto, Ph.D. 3.00
_____GUIDE TO LIVING IN BALANCE Frank S. Caprio, M.D.   2.00
_____GUIDE TO RATIONAL LIVING Albert Ellis, Ph.D. & R. Harper, Ph.D. 3.00
_____HELPING YOURSELF WITH APPLIED PSYCHOLOGY R. Henderson   2.00
_____HELPING YOURSELF WITH PSYCHIATRY Frank S. Caprio, M.D.   2.00
_____HOW TO ATTRACT GOOD LUCK A. H. Z. Carr   2.00
_____HOW TO CONTROL YOUR DESTINY Norvell   2.00
_____HOW TO DEVELOP A WINNING PERSONALITY Martin Panzer   3.00
_____HOW TO DEVELOP AN EXCEPTIONAL MEMORY Young & Gibson   3.00
_____HOW TO OVERCOME YOUR FEARS M. P. Leahy, M.D.   2.00
_____HOW YOU CAN HAVE CONFIDENCE AND POWER Les Giblin   2.00
_____HUMAN PROBLEMS & HOW TO SOLVE THEM Dr. Donald Curtis   2.00
_____I CAN Ben Sweetland   3.00
_____I WILL Ben Sweetland   2.00
_____LEFT-HANDED PEOPLE Michael Barsley   3.00
_____MAGIC IN YOUR MIND U. S. Andersen   3.00
_____MAGIC OF THINKING BIG Dr. David J. Schwartz   2.00

*The books listed above can be obtained from your book dealer or directly from
Melvin Powers. When ordering, please remit 25c per book postage & handling.
Send 25c for our illustrated catalog of self-improvement books.*

Melvin Powers

12015 Sherman Road, No. Hollywood, California 91605

WILSHIRE HORSE LOVERS' LIBRARY

_____AMATEUR HORSE BREEDER A. C. Leighton Hardman	2.00
_____AMERICAN QUARTER HORSE IN PICTURES Margaret Cabell Self	2.00
_____APPALOOSA HORSE Bill & Dona Richardson	2.00
_____ARABIAN HORSE Reginald S. Summerhays	2.00
_____ART OF WESTERN RIDING Suzanne Norton Jones	2.00
_____AT THE HORSE SHOW Margaret Cabell Self	2.00
_____BACK-YARD FOAL Peggy Jett Pittinger	2.00
_____BACK-YARD HORSE Peggy Jett Pittinger	2.00
_____BASIC DRESSAGE Jean Froissard	2.00
_____BEGINNER'S GUIDE TO HORSEBACK RIDING Sheila Wall	2.00
_____BEGINNER'S GUIDE TO THE WESTERN HORSE Natlee Kenoyer	2.00
_____BITS—THEIR HISTORY, USE AND MISUSE Louis Taylor	2.00
_____BREAKING & TRAINING THE DRIVING HORSE Doris Ganton	2.00
_____CAVALRY MANUAL OF HORSEMANSHIP Gordon Wright	2.00
_____COMPLETE TRAINING OF HORSE AND RIDER Colonel Alois Podhajsky	3.00
_____DISORDERS OF THE HORSE & WHAT TO DO ABOUT THEM E. Hanauer	2.00
_____DOG TRAINING MADE EASY & FUN John W. Kellogg	2.00
_____DRESSAGE—A study of the Finer Points in Riding Henry Wynmalen	3.00
_____DRIVING HORSES Sallie Walrond	2.00
_____EQUITATION Jean Froissard	3.00
_____FIRST AID FOR HORSES Dr. Charles H. Denning, Jr.	2.00
_____FUN OF RAISING A COLT Rubye & Frank Griffith	2.00
_____FUN ON HORSEBACK Margaret Cabell Self	3.00
_____HORSE DISEASES—Causes, Symptoms & Treatment Dr. H. G. Belschner	3.00
_____HORSE OWNER'S CONCISE GUIDE Elsie V. Hanauer	2.00
_____HORSE SELECTION & CARE FOR BEGINNERS George H. Conn	2.00
_____HORSE SENSE—A complete guide to riding and care Alan Deacon	4.00
_____HORSEBACK RIDING FOR BEGINNERS Louis Taylor	3.00
_____HORSEBACK RIDING MADE EASY & FUN Sue Henderson Coen	3.00
_____HORSES—Their Selection, Care & Handling Margaret Cabell Self	2.00
_____HOW TO BUY A BETTER HORSE & SELL THE HORSE YOU OWN	2.00
_____HOW TO ENJOY YOUR QUARTER HORSE Williard H. Porter	2.00
_____HUNTER IN PICTURES Margaret Cabell Self	2.00
_____ILLUSTRATED BOOK OF THE HORSE S. Sidney (8½" x 11½")	10.00
_____ILLUSTRATED HORSE MANAGEMENT—400 Illustrations Dr. E. Mayhew	5.00
_____ILLUSTRATED HORSE TRAINING Captain M. H. Hayes	5.00
_____ILLUSTRATED HORSEBACK RIDING FOR BEGINNERS Jeanne Mellin	2.00
_____JUMPING—Learning and Teaching Jean Froissard	2.00
_____KNOW ALL ABOUT HORSES Harry Disston	2.00
_____LAME HORSE—Causes, Symptoms & Treatment Dr. James R. Rooney	3.00
_____LAW & YOUR HORSE Edward H. Greene	3.00
_____LIPIZZANERS & THE SPANISH RIDING SCHOOL W. Reuter (4¼" x 6")	2.50
_____MORGAN HORSE IN PICTURES Margaret Cabell Self	2.00
_____MOVIE HORSES—The Fascinating Techniques of Training Anthony Amaral	2.00
_____POLICE HORSES Judith Campbell	2.00
_____PRACTICAL GUIDE TO HORSESHOEING	2.00
_____PRACTICAL GUIDE TO OWNING YOUR OWN HORSE Steven D. Price	2.00
_____PRACTICAL HORSE PSYCHOLOGY Moyra Williams	2.00
_____PROBLEM HORSES Guide for Curing Serious Behavior Habits Summerhays	2.00
_____RESCHOOLING THE THOROUGHBRED Peggy Jett Pittenger	2.00
_____RIDE WESTERN Louis Taylor	2.00
_____SCHOOLING YOUR YOUNG HORSE George Wheatley	2.00
_____STABLE MANAGEMENT FOR THE OWNER-GROOM George Wheatley	3.00
_____STALLION MANAGEMENT—A Guide for Stud Owners A. C. Hardman	2.00
_____TEACHING YOUR HORSE TO JUMP W. J. Froud	2.00
_____TRAIL HORSES & TRAIL RIDING Anne & Perry Westbrook	2.00
_____TREATING COMMON DISEASES OF YOUR HORSE Dr. George H. Conn	2.00
_____TREATING HORSE AILMENTS G. W. Serth	2.00
_____WESTERN HORSEBACK RIDING Glen Balch	2.00
_____WONDERFUL WORLD OF PONIES Peggy Jett Pittenger (8½" x 11½")	4.00
_____YOUR FIRST HORSE George C. Saunders, M.D.	2.00
_____YOUR PONY BOOK Hermann Wiederhold	2.00
_____YOUR WESTERN HORSE Nelson C. Nye	2.00

The books listed above can be obtained from your book dealer or directly from Melvin Powers. When ordering, please remit 25c per book postage & handling. Send 25c for our illustrated catalog of self-improvement books.
Melvin Powers, 12015 Sherman Road, No. Hollywood, California 91605

Notes

Notes

Notes